GREECE THROUGH THE AGES

A CONCISE GUIDE

By

Martin Miller-Yianni

The Emblem of Greece

COPYRIGHT AND ACKNOWLEDGEMENTS

Publisher: Martin Miller-Yianni, Yambol, Bulgaria

First Printed Edition 2023

ISBN 978-619-7742-27-5 (paperback)

ISBN 978-619-7742-28-2 (ePub)

A CIP catalogue record for this book is available from:

The National Register of Published Books in Bulgaria

bulevard 'Vasil Levski' 88,

1504 Sofia,

Bulgaria

Cover Photograph ('The Parthenon')

by Spencer Davis from Unsplash.com

INTRODUCTION

"Greece Through the Ages: A Concise Guide" is part of a broader series exploring the histories of various countries and remains an invaluable resource for students, inquisitive travellers, and those intrigued by the captivating history of Greece. With its well-organised structure and clear presentation, the book offers easy navigation through different historical periods and chapters, enabling readers to swiftly locate specific information.

From the ancient civilisations of Greece to contemporary developments, this book provides comprehensive coverage of the essential facets of Greece's history. It allows readers to grasp the historical context and cultural heritage of the region. The concise format makes it an ideal choice for those seeking a quick reference or an introduction to Greece's past.

Presented in a readable and accessible British English style, the book offers a comprehensive overview without compromising on accuracy or depth. This quality makes it an excellent resource for gaining knowledge about Greece's diverse historical foundations.

It's noteworthy that some chapters may recap important events. Such recapitulations are inevitable, as era transitions often share events and significant figures, reinforcing the interconnectedness of Greece's history. They serve as valuable reminders, aiding in comprehending the broader historical narrative.

Whether you aim to refresh your knowledge of a specific historical era or develop a general understanding of Greece's past, this book delivers reliable information and serves as an invaluable guide. It immerses readers in the triumphs, challenges, and cultural metamorphoses that have contributed to Greece's identity, offering a fascinating journey through time.

This book stands as an engaging and informative resource that provides a succinct yet comprehensive look at Greece's history. It remains an exceptional guide for anyone eager to explore the fascinating story of this region and gain a deeper appreciation for its rich cultural heritage.

THE FLAG OF GREECE

The Greek flag boasts a distinctive and powerful design that encapsulates the essence of the nation's rich history and cultural heritage. It features nine horizontal stripes of blue and white, alternating in colour. The blue stripes represent the sky and the sea, fundamental elements of Greece's geography and identity, while the white stripes symbolise the purity and resilience of the Greek people.

In the upper left corner of the flag, there is a blue square containing a white cross. This cross, known as the Greek cross, holds both religious and historical significance. Its design reflects Greece's strong ties to the Eastern Orthodox Church, a cornerstone of the nation's cultural and spiritual identity. Additionally, the nine stripes are said to symbolise the nine syllables of the phrase "Eleutheria i Thanatos" (Freedom or Death), a motto associated with Greece's War of Independence against the Ottoman Empire.

The contrast between the blue and white colours on the flag not only mirrors the natural beauty of Greece but also evokes a sense of clarity, freedom, and purity. The flag's design is harmonious, reflecting the nation's commitment to balance and democracy.

Officially adopted on December 22, 1978, the Greek flag is a source of immense pride for the Greek people. Its symbolism goes beyond aesthetics, serving as a visual representation of Greece's enduring spirit, cultural heritage, and the values that have shaped the nation throughout its history. The flag, with its evocative design and historical resonance, stands as a powerful emblem of Greek unity and identity.

THE LOCATION OF GREECE

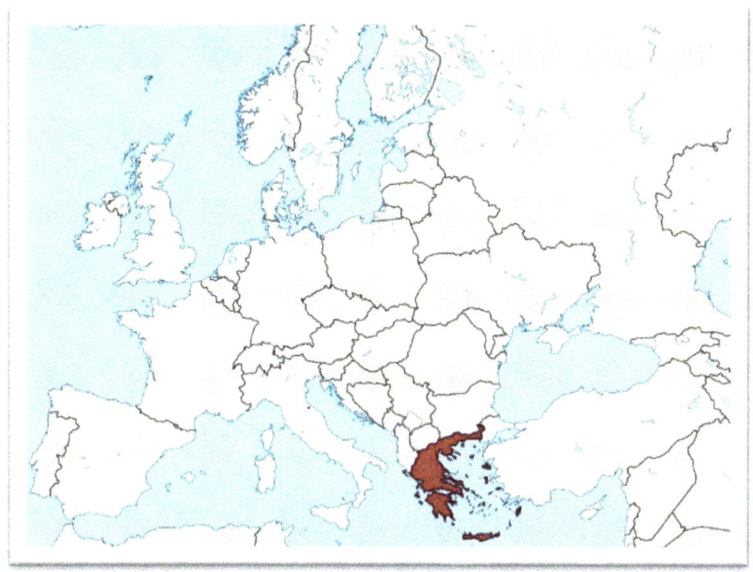

Greece, spanning about 131,957 square kilometres, is strategically located at the crossroads of Europe, Asia, and Africa. Its diverse landscape includes mountain ranges like the Pindus Mountains and Mount Olympus, fertile plains, and numerous islands in the Aegean, Ionian, and Mediterranean Seas.

The country's extensive coastline, bordered by the Aegean Sea to the east, the Ionian Sea to the west, and the Mediterranean Sea to the south, has historically influenced its culture and economic activities.

Greece shares land borders with Albania, North Macedonia, Bulgaria, and Turkey, fostering historical exchanges and cultural influences. The rivers, including the Evros and Nestos, contribute to agricultural productivity, while the climate varies from Mediterranean along the coast to alpine in certain mountainous regions.

Greece's historical legacy is shaped by civilisations such as the ancient Greeks, Romans, Byzantines, and Ottomans. Interactions with neighbouring nations, like Turkey, Albania, and Bulgaria, have influenced Greece's art, architecture, language, and traditions.

3000 – 1100 B.C.

In the southern reaches of Greece lies a cavern known as Apidima in Mani, posited to house the earliest remnants of modern humans outside the African continent, dating back a staggering 210,000 years. Scholars engage in discourse regarding whether these remains belong to archaic humans. Notably, Greece stands as a tableau showcasing the entirety of the Stone Age spectrum – Paleolithic, Mesolithic, and Neolithic. The Franchthi Cave, for instance, provides tangible evidence spanning these times.

The Franchthi Cave

Around 7,000 B.C., Neolithic settlements burgeoned in Greece, establishing themselves as the oldest in Europe by several centuries. Greece served as a conduit for the dissemination of farming practices from the Near East to the European expanse.

Greece proudly boasts hosting the inaugural advanced European civilisations, heralding the genesis of Western civilisation. The commencement transpired with the Cycladic civilisation circa 3200 B.C., succeeded by the Minoan civilisation in Crete spanning from 2700 to 1500 B.C., followed by the Mycenaean civilisation on the mainland from 1600 to 1100 B.C. These societies were endowed with written communication – Linear A for the Minoans and Linear B for the Mycenaeans.

The Mycenaeans eventually assimilated the Minoans but encountered a tumultuous collapse around 1200 B.C., coinciding with the enigmatic Late Bronze Age collapse in the region. Although the reconstruction of the political landscape from the fragmented Linear B texts proves challenging, Hittite and Egyptian records suggest the existence of a unified state under a "Great King" in mainland Greece.

During the formative epoch of Ancient Greece, spanning from 3000 to 1100 B.C., two formidable civilisations emerged, each imprinting an enduring mark on the trajectory of Hellenic history. The Minoans, flourishing on the isle of Crete, fashioned a sophisticated society epitomised by the splendour of their capital, Knossos. Renowned for its labyrinthine palace bedecked with vibrant frescoes, Knossos stood as a testament to the artistic and architectural prowess of the Minoans.

Simultaneously, on the mainland of Greece, the Mycenaeans ascended to prominence around 1600 B.C. Their citadel at Mycenae, a testament to their warrior ethos, played a central role in the unfolding narrative of Ancient Greece. King Agamemnon, a figure immortalised in Greek mythology, became synonymous with the Mycenaean civilisation and played a pivotal role in the legendary Trojan War, as chronicled in Homer's epic poems—the Iliad and the Odyssey.

King Agamemnon

The Trojan War, believed to have occurred around 1200 B.C., marked a watershed moment in this early epoch. Figures such as Achilles, Hector, and Odysseus became archetypal symbols of heroism and tragedy, weaving a rich network of myth and history. However, the aftermath of the Trojan War, coupled with various factors such as invasions, economic instability, and natural disasters, precipitated the decline of the Mycenaean civilisation.

This decline ushered in the Greek Dark Age, lasting from 1100 to 800 B.C., a period characterised by upheaval, migrations, and a simplification of material culture. Despite the challenges, this era laid the groundwork for the resurgence of Greek civilisation in the subsequent Archaic period. Trade, a hallmark of the Minoans, continued to be a driving force, fostering cultural exchange and influencing the emerging city-states.

The decipherment of Linear B, a script used by the Mycenaeans, provides insights into their administrative and economic systems. Meanwhile, archaeological excavations at sites such as Knossos and Mycenae unearth artifacts that offer glimpses into daily life, trade practices, and religious beliefs, enriching our understanding of this pivotal period.

The legacy of the Ancient Greek emergence resonates in the foundational elements of Greek culture, from religious practices to maritime traditions. As the Minoan and Mycenaean civilisations waned, they gave way to the next chapters of Greek history, setting the stage for the extraordinary developments that would unfold in the classical era and beyond.

Archaeological excavations at Knossos

Minos of Crete: Minos, the legendary king of Crete, is associated with the myth of the Minotaur and the labyrinth. His rule is often linked to the Minoan civilisation, which flourished during this period.

Mycenae: Mycenae was a powerful city-state and a key centre during the Bronze Age. The Mycenaean civilisation, known for its impressive citadel and tholos tombs, played a vital role in the development of early Greek culture.

Homer: Considered one of the greatest poets of ancient Greece, Homer's epic poems, the Iliad and the Odyssey, are foundational works that provide insights into the heroic age and early Greek society.

Troy: Troy, the city immortalised in the epic poems of Homer, is famous for the Trojan War. The legendary conflict between the Greeks and Trojans, as described in the Iliad, is a central event of this era.

Pylos: Pylos, a significant Mycenaean palace and administrative centre, was excavated by archaeologist Carl Blegen. The tablets found at Pylos contain the Linear B script, providing valuable information about Mycenaean language and society.

Theseus: Theseus, a mythical hero and king of Athens, is associated with deeds such as the slaying of the Minotaur. His adventures are often intertwined with the early myths and legends of Greece.

Knossos: Knossos, located on the island of Crete, was a major Minoan city. The palace of Knossos, attributed to King Minos, showcases advanced architectural features and a complex layout.

Agamemnon: Agamemnon, a legendary Mycenaean king, played a central role in the Trojan War. His story is depicted in the works of Homer and later Greek tragedies, such as Aeschylus' "Oresteia."

CHAPTER 2: GODS AND HEROES

1100 – 800 B.C.

Through the subsequent era, spanning from 1100 to 800 B.C., Ancient Greece found itself immersed in a realm of myths and legends—a period encapsulated by the intertwining narratives of gods and heroes. The aftermath of the Greek Dark Age witnessed the gradual resurgence of cultural and societal dynamics, with the mythological landscape taking centre stage.

As communities reorganised and the Greek city-states began to re-emerge, a rich mixture of myths and legends took root, woven into the very fabric of daily life. The pantheon of gods and goddesses, influenced by both Minoan and Mycenaean religious traditions, became central figures in the collective imagination of the Greek people.

The gods, with their divine personalities and powers, played a multifaceted role in the lives of the Greeks. The Olympian deities, including Zeus, Hera, Athena, and Apollo, presided over various aspects of existence, from the affairs of state to the arts and wisdom. These divine beings became the focal point of religious practices, rituals, and festivals, shaping the spiritual landscape of the emerging Greek city-states.

The God Zeus Battling Typhon

Simultaneously, the realm of heroes unfolded—a world where mortal and divine intertwined. The epic poems of Homer, the Iliad, and the Odyssey, served as monumental literary achievements that immortalised the exploits of heroic figures. Achilles, the mighty warrior of the Trojan War; Odysseus, the cunning hero on a perilous journey; and the valiant Hector, each played a role in shaping the heroic ethos of early Greece.

The Bust of Homer

Mythological tales not only entertained but also conveyed cultural values, moral lessons, and societal norms. These stories, passed down orally from generation to generation, became a vital part of the Greek identity. The vivid narratives of gods and heroes provided a framework for understanding the world, exploring themes of heroism, hubris, and the complex interplay between mortals and the divine.

The archaeological remnants of this period further illuminate the enduring impact of these myths. Artifacts adorned with depictions of gods and heroes attest to the significance of these tales in the daily lives of the ancient Greeks. As the Greek city-states continued to evolve, the mythological heritage laid the foundation for the flourishing of classical Greek culture, philosophy, and the arts, leaving an indelible mark on the trajectory of Western civilisation.

Zeus: Zeus, the king of the gods, played a central role in Greek mythology. As the god of the sky and thunder, his stories and exploits were woven into the fabric of Greek religious beliefs. Mount Olympus was considered his divine abode.

Heracles (Hercules): Heracles, the most celebrated hero in Greek mythology, was known for his incredible strength and his twelve labours. His exploits and adventures were legendary, making him a popular figure in ancient Greek culture.

Achilles: Achilles, a hero of the Trojan War, was famed for his exceptional prowess in battle. The epic poem, the Iliad, attributed to Homer, narrates his deeds and tragic fate.

Athena: Athena, the goddess of wisdom and warfare, was highly revered in ancient Greece. The city of Athens was named after her, and she played a significant role in various myths, including the contest with Poseidon for the patronage of Athens.

Odysseus: Odysseus, the hero of Homer's Odyssey, undertook a perilous journey home after the Trojan War. His cunning and resourcefulness were key to overcoming the challenges he faced.

Hera: Hera, the queen of the gods and the wife of Zeus, featured prominently in Greek mythology. Her relationship with Zeus and her role in various myths, including the Twelve Labours of Heracles, added depth to the pantheon.

Perseus: Perseus, a hero known for slaying the Gorgon Medusa, embarked on quests that showcased his bravery and resourcefulness. His lineage connects him to other famous figures in Greek mythology.

Artemis: Artemis, the goddess of the hunt and wilderness, was also associated with the moon. Her stories often depicted her as an independent and fierce deity, protecting the natural world.

The Underworld (Hades): The concept of the Underworld, ruled by Hades, played a significant role in Greek mythology. It was believed to be the realm of the dead, and myths surrounding it, such as the story of Orpheus and Eurydice, explored themes of mortality and the afterlife.

Dionysus: Dionysus, the god of wine, fertility, and revelry, was a complex deity associated with both joyous celebration and wild, unpredictable behaviour. His worship was marked by festivals and theatrical performances.

800 – 500 B.C.

Following the collapse of the Mycenaean civilisation, a period known as the Greek Dark Ages unfolded, shrouded in the absence of written records. The conclusion of this era is conventionally marked in 776 B.C., deemed the inaugural year of the Olympic Games. Attributed to Homer in the 7th or 8th centuries B.C., the Iliad and the Odyssey stand as foundational texts in Western literature. Subsequent to the Dark Ages, diverse kingdoms and city-states emerged across the Greek peninsula, extending their influence to the Black Sea, Southern Italy (Magna Graecia), and Asia Minor. This time witnessed the flourishing of classical Greece, showcasing advancements in architecture, drama, science, mathematics, and philosophy. In 508 B.C., Cleisthenes introduced the world's first democratic system in Athens.

In the era spanning from 800 to 500 B.C., the landscape of Ancient Greece underwent a transformative phase marked by the ascendancy of city-states and the genesis of democratic ideals. This period, commonly referred to as the Archaic Age, laid the groundwork for the political, social, and cultural innovations that would sculpt the course of Greek history.

As the Greek Dark Age gave way to renewed vitality, the city-states, or polis, emerged as the focal points of Greek society. Noteworthy among them were Athens, Sparta, Corinth, and

Thebes, each evolving with distinct political structures and civic identities. The city-state transcended mere geographical boundaries; it embodied a community of citizens actively engaged in shaping the destiny of their polis.

Athens, in particular, stood as a beacon of democratic experimentation. The reforms of leaders such as Solon and Cleisthenes formed the bedrock of a participatory political system that would eventually become the hallmark of Athenian democracy. Citizens, primarily adult males, were afforded the opportunity to participate in decision-making through an assembly known as the Ekklesia. This democratic experiment, while imperfect by modern standards, represented a groundbreaking departure from earlier forms of governance.

In stark contrast, the city-state of Sparta embraced a unique system prioritising military prowess and discipline. The Spartan constitution, attributed to the legendary lawgiver Lycurgus, sought to fashion a society of highly disciplined citizens focused on the collective welfare of the state. Sparta's military might and emphasis on communal living stood in stark contrast to the more individualistic and democratic ethos of Athens.

This period also bore witness to significant cultural achievements. The flourishing of the arts, literature, and philosophy reflected the dynamism of the city-states. Luminaries such as the poet Sappho in Lesbos and the philosopher Thales in Miletus contributed to the intellectual ferment of the time.

Bronze Statue of the Warrier Sparta
Trade and colonisation played a pivotal role in connecting the
city-states and fostering cultural exchange. The Mediterranean

evolved into a network of maritime routes, facilitating the exchange of goods, ideas, and cultural practices. The agora, or marketplace, not only served as an economic hub but also as a space for social interaction, political discourse, and the exchange of diverse perspectives.

As the city-states continued to evolve, the birth of democracy in Athens and the distinctive political structures of other poleis set the stage for the classical period. The legacy of this transformative era resonates through the annals of Western political thought, laying the groundwork for the enduring principles of citizenship and governance.

Solon: Solon, an Athenian statesman and lawmaker, played a crucial role in the early development of Athenian democracy. He enacted political and economic reforms to address social inequalities and laid the foundation for future democratic governance.

Lycurgus: Lycurgus, the legendary lawgiver of Sparta, was credited with establishing the Spartan constitution and shaping the militaristic society of ancient Sparta. His reforms aimed at creating a disciplined and resilient city-state.

Athens: Athens, the capital of Attica, emerged as a significant cultural and political centre during this period. Known for its democratic experiment and cultural achievements, Athens became a powerhouse among the Greek city-states.

Sparta: Sparta, a powerful military city-state in the Peloponnese, was renowned for its disciplined and formidable army. The Spartan military system and way of life were distinctive and played a major role in Greek history.

Peisistratos: Peisistratos, a tyrant of Athens, rose to power in the early 6th century B.C. Despite the negative connotations of the term "tyrant," Peisistratos is often credited with fostering economic and cultural growth in Athens.

Corinth: Corinth, a major maritime and trade centre, played a crucial role in the economic networks of the ancient Greek world. The city-state was strategically located and became a significant player in regional politics.

The Delian League: The Delian League, initially formed as an alliance against the Persians, later became an Athenian-led confederation. However, over time, it transformed into an empire with Athens exerting dominance over member city-states.

Cleisthenes: Cleisthenes, an Athenian statesman, is often referred to as the "Father of Athenian Democracy." His reforms in the late 6th century B.C. laid the groundwork for the democratic system that would characterise Athens.

Thebes: Thebes, located in Boeotia, rose to prominence in the 5th century B.C. It played a significant role in various conflicts, including the Peloponnesian War and the Battle of Leuctra.

Miletus: Miletus, an influential city-state in Ionia, was known for its philosophical and scientific contributions. It was a hub of intellectual activity and played a role in the early development of Greek philosophy.

500 – 449 B.C.

In the records of history, the period between 500 and 449 B.C. thrust Ancient Greece onto the international stage, setting the scene for the dramatic conflict known as the Persian Wars. This period of profound geopolitical upheaval marked a crucial chapter in Greek history, as the city-states coalesced to confront the formidable external threat posed by the expansive Persian Empire.

The Persian Wars unfolded as a series of conflicts between the Greek city-states, chiefly spearheaded by Athens and Sparta, and the formidable Persian Empire under the rule of King Darius I and later his successor, Xerxes I. The initial spark ignited with the Ionian Revolt (499–494 B.C.), where Greek-inhabited cities in Asia Minor sought independence from Persian rule. Athens, in a bold move, extended support to the Ionian rebels, marking the commencement of a protracted conflict with the Persian Empire.

The iconic Battle of Marathon in 490 B.C. emerged as the inaugural major confrontation. Despite being outnumbered, the Athenian forces, under the leadership of Miltiades, secured a decisive victory against the Persian army. The legendary marathon run symbolised a pivotal moment in the defence of Greek autonomy, with the Athenians successfully repelling the Persian invasion.

Scene at the Battle of Marathon

A decade later, Xerxes I orchestrated a colossal invasion in 480 B.C., prompting the city-states to unite in an alliance known as the Hellenic League. The ensuing battles, including the renowned last stand at Thermopylae and the naval triumph at Salamis, highlighted the resilience and strategic acumen of the Greeks. Themistocles, the Athenian statesman and general, played a pivotal role in orchestrating the Greek victory at the Battle of Salamis, a turning point that thwarted Persian naval dominance.

The subsequent Battle of Plataea in 479 B.C. and the naval Battle of Mycale dealt final blows to the Persian forces, solidifying Greek success in repelling external aggression. The Delian League, established in the aftermath, underscored the commitment among city-states to prevent any future Persian incursions.

This era of conflict resonated profoundly in the trajectory of Greek history. The unity forged during the Persian Wars laid the groundwork for the ascendance of Athens as a dominant naval power and the transformation of the Delian League into an Athenian-led maritime empire. The victories also instilled a sense of pride and confidence among the Greeks, influencing cultural and artistic expressions.

Chronicled by historians such as Herodotus, the Persian Wars demonstrated the significance of collective action in the face of external threats and left an enduring legacy on the concept of democracy and the values of freedom and autonomy in Western political thought.

Darius I: Darius I, the Persian king, initiated the first Persian invasion of Greece in 490 B.C., culminating in the Battle of Marathon. His aspirations for expanding the Persian Empire into Greece set the stage for the larger conflict.

Miltiades: Miltiades, an Athenian general, played a pivotal role in the Battle of Marathon. His strategic acumen and leadership were crucial in securing a surprising victory for the Athenians against the Persians.

Xerxes I: Xerxes I, the son of Darius, led the second Persian invasion of Greece. His forces clashed with the Greeks in iconic battles such as Thermopylae and Salamis. Xerxes sought revenge for the Persian defeat at Marathon.

Leonidas I, the king of Sparta, led the famous stand of the 300 Spartans at the Battle of Thermopylae in 480 B.C. Despite being defeated, their heroic resistance became a symbol of Greek determination.

Themistocles: Themistocles, an Athenian statesman and general, played a key role in the Battle of Salamis. He advocated for the naval strategy that ultimately led to a significant Greek victory over the Persian fleet.

Artemisia I of Caria: Artemisia, a queen and naval commander in the service of Xerxes, stood out for her leadership during the Battle of Salamis. Her tactical advice was respected even by the Greeks.

Battle of Plataea: The Battle of Plataea in 479 B.C. marked the decisive land engagement between the Greeks and Persians. The Greek forces, led by Spartan Pausanias, achieved a significant victory, further securing Greek independence.

Themistocles' Long Walls: Themistocles, recogniseng the importance of naval power, initiated the construction of the Long Walls connecting Athens to its port, Piraeus. This move allowed Athens to maintain its naval strength during the wars.

The Delian League: Formed in the aftermath of the Persian Wars, the Delian League was an alliance of Greek city-states aimed at preventing further Persian invasions. Athens emerged as a dominant force within the league.

Peace of Callias: The Peace of Callias, a supposed peace treaty between Athens and Persia, marked the end of hostilities between the two powers. However, its historical authenticity is debated among scholars.

CHAPTER 5: GOLDEN AGE OF ATHENS

448 – 404 B.C.

Conflicts among Greek states persisted, culminating in the devastating Peloponnesian War (431–404 B.C.), ultimately won by Sparta and resulting in the waning of Athens as the dominant power.

In the period spanning from 448 to 404 B.C., Ancient Greece witnessed the pinnacle of cultural and intellectual achievement during the Golden Age of Athens. Guided by the visionary leadership of statesman Pericles, Athens emerged as a shining beacon of democracy, artistic brilliance, and intellectual innovation, leaving an indelible mark on the chronicles of Western civilisation.

Pericles, a prominent figure in Athenian politics, implemented a series of reforms that fortified the democratic foundations of the city-state. His leadership, characterised by eloquence and strategic acumen, ushered in an era of unparalleled cultural vibrancy. Pericles envisioned Athens as an exemplar of democratic governance, where citizens actively participated in decision-making, shaping the destiny of the polis.

The Visionary Statesman Pericles

The Parthenon, an enduring symbol of Athens, stands as a testament to the architectural brilliance of the time. Pericles commissioned the construction of this iconic temple atop the Acropolis, dedicated to the goddess Athena. Crafted by architects Ictinus and Callicrates and adorned with sculptures by Phidias, the Parthenon embodied the harmonious fusion of aesthetic beauty and mathematical precision, epitomising the ideals of classical Greek art and architecture.

The Parthenon

Theatre flourished during this period, with playwrights such as Aeschylus, Sophocles, and Euripides producing timeless dramas that delved into the complexities of human existence. The Dionysian festivals, particularly the City Dionysia, provided a platform for the performance of tragedies and comedies, captivating audiences with profound narratives and satirical wit.

Philosophy reached new heights through the teachings of Socrates, Plato, and Aristotle. These intellectual giants engaged in profound inquiries into ethics, metaphysics, and epistemology, laying the foundations for Western philosophy. The Socratic method, an enduring pedagogical approach, exemplified the pursuit of knowledge through dialogue and questioning.

In the realm of politics, Pericles' Funeral Oration, as chronicled by Thucydides, encapsulated the essence of Athenian democracy. Delivered in honour of those who fell in the Peloponnesian War, the oration celebrated the virtues of Athenian society, emphasising individual freedoms, collective responsibility, and the pursuit of excellence.

Ancient Greece bore witness to the fracturing of its unity as the Peloponnesian War unfolded, casting a shadow over the once-cohesive city-states. This protracted and devastating conflict between Athens and its allies in the Delian League, and Sparta and its allies in the Peloponnesian League, marked a tragic chapter in Greek history, leading to the erosion of Greek unity.

Chronicled by the historian Thucydides, the Peloponnesian War stemmed from longstanding tensions between Athens, the naval power dominating the Delian League, and Sparta, the formidable land power leading the Peloponnesian League. The underlying causes encompassed political differences, economic competition, and the contentious issue of Athenian imperialism.

The conflict unfolded in three main phases: the Archidamian War (431–421 B.C.), the Sicilian Expedition (415–413 B.C.), and the Ionian or Decelean War (413–404 B.C.). The Archidamian War witnessed a series of intermittent conflicts, marked by battles and truces, as both sides sought strategic advantages.

The Sicilian Expedition, a disastrous venture for Athens, strained its resources and weakened its position. The Ionian War, centred around the fortified city of Decelea and the island of Euboea, intensified the conflict, culminating in the ultimate downfall of Athens.

The war had profound consequences on the Greek city-states. Internal strife and external pressures exposed the vulnerabilities of the democratic experiment in Athens. The devastating Plague of Athens in 429 B.C. compounded the city's woes, claiming the lives of many, including the revered Pericles.

The rivalry between Athens and Sparta ignited tensions that reverberated across the Greek world, fracturing alliances and pitting city-states against each other. The once-shared cultural and political ideals gave way to suspicion and conflict, eroding the sense of a united Hellenic identity.

The conclusion of the war in 404 B.C. marked the fall of Athens and the ascendancy of Sparta. The terms of the Peace of Nicias and later the harsh terms of the Thirty Tyrants, imposed by Sparta on Athens, signified the end of Athenian hegemony. The dream of a united Greece lay shattered, replaced by a landscape of fractured city-states and shifting power dynamics.

Amidst the ruins of unity, the Peloponnesian War left behind a legacy of lessons. Thucydides' account of the war stands as a seminal work in the history of historiography, providing insights into the complexities of human nature, power dynamics, and the consequences of war. The war's impact on Greek political thought, as evidenced in the works of philosophers like Plato, reflected a collective grappling with the challenges of governance and the fragility of democratic ideals.

The Peloponnesian War, while marking a period of decline and disunity for the Greek city-states, also paved the way for subsequent developments in politics, philosophy, and historical understanding. Its echoes resonate through the ages, serving as a cautionary tale about the fragility of unity and the enduring complexities of human interactions on the stage of history.

King of Sparta at the Court of Archidamas by Thucydides

Pericles: Pericles, an influential statesman, orator, and general, played a central role in shaping the Golden Age of Athens. He promoted democracy, sponsored the construction of the Parthenon, and led Athens through a period of prosperity.

Parthenon and Acropolis: Under the guidance of Pericles, the construction of the Parthenon atop the Acropolis in Athens took place. This iconic temple dedicated to Athena is a symbol of classical Greek architecture and artistic achievement.

Aspasia: Aspasia, a well-educated and influential woman, was the companion of Pericles. Known for her intellect and charm, she played a role in Athenian political and cultural life.

Euripides: Euripides, a prominent playwright, was active during the Golden Age. His tragedies, such as "Medea" and "The Bacchae," reflected the intellectual and emotional depth of Greek drama.

Sophocles: Sophocles, another renowned playwright, contributed significantly to Greek theatre. His tragedies, including "Oedipus Rex" and "Antigone," are considered masterpieces of classical literature.

Herodotus: Herodotus, often referred to as the "Father of History," wrote "Histories" during this period. His work is an account of the Greco-Persian Wars and other historical events.

Thucydides: Thucydides, a historian and contemporary of Herodotus, wrote "History of the Peloponnesian War," providing a detailed and analytical account of the conflict between Athens and Sparta.

Peloponnesian War: The Peloponnesian War (431–404 B.C.) was a protracted conflict between Athens and Sparta, leading to the decline of Athenian power. The war had a profound impact on the Greek city-states.

Plato: Plato, a philosopher and student of Socrates, emerged during the later years of the Golden Age. His philosophical dialogues, including "The Republic," explored political and ethical ideas.

Socrates: Socrates, a philosopher and teacher of Plato, questioned conventional wisdom and encouraged critical thinking. His method of questioning, known as the Socratic method, influenced classical Greek philosophy.

Hippocrates: Hippocrates, often called the "Father of Medicine," lived during this period. His ethical approach to medicine and the compilation of the Hippocratic Corpus laid the foundations for Western medicine.

336 – 323 B.C.

During the transformative period from 336 to 323 B.C., Ancient Greece bore witness to the extraordinary rise of Macedonian power under the indomitable leadership of Alexander the Great. This era, known as the Macedonian Ascendancy, marked an era of unparalleled conquests and cultural amalgamation that reshaped the geopolitical landscape of the ancient world.

Alexander the Great

Alexander, the son of King Philip II of Macedon, ascended to the throne in 336 B.C. following the assassination of his father. From the outset, he displayed prodigious military and strategic acumen, earning him a place among history's most legendary commanders. His vision extended far beyond the borders of Macedonia, propelling him to embark on a relentless campaign of conquest that stretched from Greece to Egypt, Persia, and beyond.

The Battle of Chaeronea in 338 B.C., where the young Alexander served as a commander under his father, marked an early triumph for Macedon over the combined forces of Athens and Thebes. This victory solidified Macedonian dominance in Greece and set the stage for Alexander's ambitions beyond the Hellenic world.

Alexander's conquests commenced in earnest in 334 B.C. with the invasion of the Persian Empire. The Battle of Granicus saw Alexander's forces decisively defeating the Persian army, initiating a series of campaigns that would culminate in the fall of the Achaemenid Empire. The pivotal Battle of Issus in 333 B.C. and the subsequent conquest of the strategic city of Tyre in 332 B.C. further established Alexander's dominance in the eastern Mediterranean.

The crowning achievement came with the conquest of Egypt in 332 B.C., where Alexander was hailed as a liberator by the Egyptians. The founding of the city of Alexandria exemplified Alexander's strategic vision, creating a hub of commerce and culture that would endure for centuries.

The most celebrated phase of Alexander's conquests unfolded in the heart of the Persian Empire. The Battle of Gaugamela in 331 B.C. witnessed the decisive defeat of Persian King Darius III, solidifying Alexander's control over Persia. The cities of Babylon and Persepolis fell into Macedonian hands, symbolising the end of Persian rule.

Battle of Gaugamela

The epic march through the Persian Empire continued into Central Asia and the Indian subcontinent, pushing the boundaries of the known world. The Battle of the Hydaspes in 326 B.C., against King Porus of India, showcased Alexander's tactical brilliance, but the wearied and homesick army eventually compelled him to turn back.

Alexander's untimely death in 323 B.C., at the age of 32, marked the conclusion of an era. The vast empire he had forged, stretching from Greece to Egypt, Persia, and beyond, faced the challenges of succession. The Hellenistic period emerged, characterised by the blending of Greek and Persian cultures, known as Hellenisation.

The legacy of Alexander's conquests extended beyond mere territorial expansion. The fusion of Greek and Eastern cultures, exemplified by the Hellenistic era, shaped the artistic, scientific, and philosophical currents of the time. The spread of Greek language, institutions, and ideas laid the foundation for the later Roman and Byzantine civilisations.

The Macedonian Ascendancy, under Alexander the Great, stands as a testament to the transformative power of vision, strategy, and military prowess. While his conquests altered the course of history, the cultural and intellectual fusion that ensued reflected the enduring impact of the Hellenistic legacy on the civilisations that followed.

A SUMMARY OF KEY EVENTS, PEOPLE AND PLACES DURING THIS ERA

Alexander the Great: Alexander, the son of King Philip II of Macedon, ascended to the throne in 336 B.C. He became one of history's most successful military commanders, conquering an expansive empire that stretched from Greece to Egypt and as far east as India.

Philip II: Philip II of Macedon, the father of Alexander, was a skilled military strategist who laid the groundwork for his son's conquests. His military reforms and diplomatic efforts set the stage for the rise of Macedon.

Battle of Chaeronea: In 338 B.C., Philip II secured a decisive victory at the Battle of Chaeronea, solidifying Macedonian dominance over Greece. This marked the end of the city-states' autonomy and the establishment of Macedonian hegemony.

Hephaestion: Hephaestion, a close companion and friend of Alexander, played a significant role in his conquests. His friendship with Alexander was widely celebrated, and his death deeply affected the king.

Siege of Tyre: The Siege of Tyre in 332 B.C. was a pivotal moment in Alexander's campaign in the Persian Empire. The strategic capture of the island city demonstrated his military ingenuity.

Darius III: Darius III, the last Achaemenid king of Persia, faced multiple defeats at the hands of Alexander. The Battle of Issus (333 B.C.) and the Battle of Gaugamela (331 B.C.) were crucial clashes between their forces.

The Gordian Knot: In 333 B.C., Alexander famously encountered the Gordian Knot, an intricate knot tied to a chariot in Gordium. He "cut the knot" with his sword, fulfilling the prophecy that the person who could unravel it would rule Asia.

Persepolis: After defeating Darius III, Alexander captured and later burned the Achaemenid capital, Persepolis, in 330 B.C. The event symbolised the fall of the Persian Empire.

Bucephalus: Bucephalus, the beloved horse of Alexander, accompanied him in many battles, including the conquest of Persia. The horse's loyalty and courage became legendary.

Death of Alexander: Alexander the Great died in 323 B.C. in Babylon, at the age of 32. His death led to a period of political and military turmoil known as the Wars of the Diadochi, as his generals vied for control.

CHAPTER 7: HELLENISTIC ERA

323 – 146 B.C.

In the aftermath of Alexander the Great's untimely demise in 323 B.C., the Hellenistic Era unfolded, marking a period of profound cultural exchange and political realignment. This era, spanning from 323 to 146 B.C., witnessed the dissemination of Greek influence across the vast territories conquered by Alexander, giving rise to a diverse and interconnected world shaped by Hellenistic ideals.

Following Alexander's death, his vast empire was divided among his generals in the Wars of the Diadochi, leading to the formation of several successor states known as the Diadochi Kingdoms. Ptolemy secured control over Egypt, Seleucus over Mesopotamia and Persia, Antigonus over Asia Minor, and Cassander over Macedonia and Greece. These Hellenistic kingdoms became centres of power, each striving to maintain and expand its influence.

One of the notable legacies of the Hellenistic Era was the establishment of Alexandria as a cultural and intellectual hub. The Library of Alexandria, founded during the reign of Ptolemy II, became a beacon of knowledge, attracting scholars from across the Hellenistic world. This period saw significant advancements in fields such as mathematics, astronomy, and medicine, with notable figures like Euclid, Eratosthenes, and Herophilus contributing to the intellectual ferment.

Ptolemy II

Cultural syncretism emerged as a defining feature of the Hellenistic world. Greek traditions blended with local customs, particularly in regions with rich historical and cultural backgrounds. This fusion of Greek and Eastern elements gave rise to unique art forms, architectural styles, and religious practices. The Greco-Bactrian Kingdom in Central Asia and the Indo-Greek Kingdom in the Indian subcontinent exemplified this synthesis, showcasing the intermingling of Greek and local cultures.

The Hellenistic kingdoms faced external threats from emerging powers such as the Seleucid Empire's clashes with the Maurya Empire in India and the expansion of the Roman Republic in the west. The Battle of Ipsus in 301 B.C., where the Diadochi engaged in a decisive conflict, resulted in the further fragmentation of Alexander's empire.

The maritime prowess of the Hellenistic kingdoms facilitated extensive trade networks across the Mediterranean and beyond, fostering economic prosperity and cultural exchange. The establishment of the Silk Road, connecting the Mediterranean with Asia, exemplified the interconnectedness of the Hellenistic world.

Despite the cultural and economic vibrancy, internal conflicts and power struggles continued to characterise the Hellenistic kingdoms. The series of conflicts known as the Syrian Wars, involving the Seleucid and Ptolemaic Empires, underscored the enduring challenges of maintaining stability in the wake of Alexander's conquests.

The Hellenistic Era drew to a close with the expansion of the Roman Republic, culminating in the Battle of Corinth in 146 B.C. The Roman victory marked the end of Hellenistic independence, as Greece became a Roman province, and the

Hellenistic legacy became an integral part of the Roman Empire's cultural makeup.

The Hellenistic Era, while witnessing the fragmentation of Alexander's empire, left an enduring legacy of cultural diffusion, intellectual flourishing, and artistic innovation. The blending of Greek, Persian, Egyptian, and Indian elements shaped the cultural landscape of the eastern Mediterranean and beyond, laying the groundwork for the subsequent development of Western civilisation.

A SUMMARY OF KEY EVENTS, PEOPLE AND PLACES DURING THIS ERA

Ptolemy I Soter: Ptolemy I, a general of Alexander, became the ruler of Egypt. The Ptolemaic Dynasty, which he founded, would govern Egypt for centuries during the Hellenistic period.

Seleucus I Nicator: Seleucus I, another of Alexander's generals, founded the Seleucid Empire, encompassing a vast territory from Anatolia to the Iranian Plateau. The Seleucids played a key role in the spread of Hellenistic culture in the East.

Antigonus I Monophthalmus: Antigonus I, a general and successor of Alexander, established the Antigonid Dynasty in Macedonia. His descendants ruled over Macedon and parts of Greece.

Hellenistic Kingdoms: The Hellenistic Era saw the fragmentation of Alexander's empire into three major successor states: the Ptolemaic Kingdom in Egypt, the Seleucid Empire in the East, and the Antigonid Kingdom in Macedon.

Epicurus: Epicurus, a philosopher, founded the school of philosophy known as Epicureanism. His teachings focused on achieving happiness through the pursuit of simple pleasures and the avoidance of pain.

Zeno of Citium: Zeno, the founder of Stoicism, developed a philosophy that emphasised virtue, reason, and the acceptance of fate. Stoicism became influential throughout the Hellenistic and Roman periods.

Euclid: Euclid, a mathematician based in Alexandria, compiled "Elements," a comprehensive textbook on geometry that became a foundational work in mathematics for centuries.

Archimedes: Archimedes, a mathematician and inventor in Syracuse, made significant contributions to mathematics and physics. His inventions and discoveries include the Archimedean screw and principles of buoyancy.

Berenice II: Berenice II, a queen of Egypt from the Ptolemaic Dynasty, is known for her support of cultural and scientific endeavours. The famous "Coma Berenices" in astronomy is named after her.

Hannibal Barca: Hannibal, the Carthaginian military commander, rose to prominence during the Second Punic War against Rome. His tactical brilliance, including the famous crossing of the Alps, left a lasting impact.

Battle of Ipsus: The Battle of Ipsus in 301 B.C. marked a significant conflict among the Diadochi, resulting in the partition of Alexander's empire among the victors.

Commencing around 200 B.C., the Roman Republic increasingly immersed itself in Greek affairs, sparking a sequence of conflicts with Macedon. The Battle of Pydna in 168 B.C. signified the demise of Antigonid power in Greece, leading to the annexation of Macedonia as a Roman province in 146 B.C., while the rest of Greece became a Roman protectorate.

This process culminated in 27 B.C. when the Roman emperor Augustus incorporated the remaining Greek territories, forming the senatorial province of Achaea. Despite their military dominance, the Romans held a deep admiration for Greek culture, evident in Horace's famous statement: "Graecia capta ferum victorem cepit" ("Greece, although captured, took its wild conqueror captive"). Roman authors, including Virgil drawing inspiration from Homer, and figures such as Scipio Africanus delving into philosophy, reflected the profound impact of Greek culture on Rome. Emperors like Nero and Hadrian maintained a strong affinity for Greek traditions, with Hadrian even serving as an eponymous archon of Athens before ascending to the throne.

Greek-speaking communities in the Hellenised East played a vital role in disseminating early Christianity in the 2nd and 3rd centuries. Notably, St. Paul, one of Christianity's early leaders and writers, was Greek-speaking. The New Testament, written in Greek, reflects the significance of Greek churches in early Christianity, as seen in Corinthians, Thessalonians, Philippians, and the Revelation of St. John of Patmos.

Roman Emperor Augustus

Despite the rise of Christianity, many parts of Greece clung to paganism. Ancient Greek religious practices endured until the late 4th century A.D. when Emperor Theodosius I outlawed them in 391–392. The last recorded Olympic Games were in

393, and numerous temples suffered damage or destruction in the ensuing century. Paganism persisted in Athens and rural areas well into the sixth century and even later in some regions.

During these times, ancient Greece underwent a profound shift in its political landscape as it fell under the dominion of Rome. This period, encompassing the Rise of Rome and Greece under Imperial Rule, marked the convergence of Hellenistic and Roman cultures, influencing the trajectory of both civilisations.

The Roman victory in the Battle of Corinth in 146 B.C. marked the end of Hellenistic independence as Greece became a province of the expanding Roman Republic. The Roman conquest brought about a transformation in political structures, with Greek city-states losing their autonomy and being incorporated into the administrative framework of the Roman Empire. Despite the loss of political sovereignty, Greek culture, philosophy, and art continued to flourish under Roman rule, shaping the cultural identity of the eastern Mediterranean.

During the early years of Roman rule, Greece maintained a degree of cultural distinctiveness. Roman leaders, particularly those with an appreciation for Greek culture, embraced Hellenistic traditions. This cultural affinity was epitomised by figures like the Roman general Sulla, who, despite his military campaigns in Greece, admired Greek philosophy and literature.

The city of Athens, although diminished in political significance, retained its status as a cultural and intellectual centre. Roman emperors such as Hadrian demonstrated a particular fondness for Greek culture, contributing to the restoration and embellishment of Athens. The construction of the Library of Hadrian and the completion of the Temple of Olympian Zeus were among the architectural projects that showcased the enduring influence of Greek aesthetics.

The emergence of the Roman Empire ushered in an era of relative stability in the eastern Mediterranean. The Pax Romana (Roman Peace) provided an environment conducive to economic prosperity and cultural exchange. Greek cities, now integrated into the Roman administrative apparatus, became vital hubs of trade, commerce, and intellectual activity.

Greek philosophy continued to thrive during this period, with notable philosophers such as Epictetus, a Stoic philosopher born in Hierapolis (modern-day Pamukkale, Turkey), contributing to the philosophical discourse of the time. The melding of Greek and Roman philosophical traditions became evident in the works of philosophers like Plutarch, who sought to reconcile the two cultural streams.

The spread of Christianity, originating in the eastern Mediterranean, gained prominence during the Roman Imperial period. The Apostle Paul's missionary journeys and the early Christian communities that emerged in places like Corinth and Thessaloniki played a pivotal role in the dissemination of Christian teachings.

As the Roman Empire faced internal challenges and external threats, the administrative and cultural integration of the Greek East into the broader Roman context became more pronounced. The division of the Roman Empire into the Western and Eastern Roman Empires in 285 A.D. further solidified the distinct identity of the eastern provinces, which would eventually evolve into the Byzantine Empire.

By the end of this period in 330 A.D., when Emperor Constantine I established Constantinople (modern-day Istanbul) as the new capital of the Roman Empire, the influence of Greek culture had become an integral part of the Byzantine identity. The Byzantine Empire, while distinctly Roman, carried forward the Hellenistic legacy, ensuring the continued vitality of Greek traditions in the centuries to come.

Roman Emperor Constantine I

The closure of the Neoplatonic Academy of Athens by Emperor Justinian in 529 is often considered the symbolic end of antiquity, though evidence suggests the academy continued activities for some time. Some remote areas, like the southeastern Peloponnese, clung to paganism until the 10th century A.D.

Gaius Marius: Gaius Marius, a military and political figure, enacted significant military reforms during the late Roman Republic. His professionalisation of the Roman army had long-lasting effects.

Lucius Cornelius Sulla: Sulla, a general and statesman, played a crucial role in Roman politics during the late Republic. His march on Rome and subsequent dictatorship marked a turning point in Roman political history.

Julius Caesar: Julius Caesar, a military genius and politician, played a key role in the demise of the Roman Republic. His crossing of the Rubicon River and subsequent civil war led to his dictatorship and laid the groundwork for the Roman Empire.

First Triumvirate: The First Triumvirate, formed by Julius Caesar, Pompey the Great, and Marcus Crassus, was a political alliance that helped shape Roman politics in the late Republic. The eventual breakdown of the triumvirate contributed to the series of civil wars.

Cicero: Cicero, a prominent orator and statesman, was a leading figure in Roman politics during the late Republic. His speeches and writings provide valuable insights into the political and intellectual climate of the time.

Cleopatra VII: Cleopatra, the last Pharaoh of Egypt, was romantically involved with Julius Caesar and later Mark Antony. Her relationships with Roman leaders influenced the dynamics of the late Republic.

Ides of March: The Ides of March in 44 B.C. marked the assassination of Julius Caesar. The conspirators, including Brutus and Cassius, sought to prevent what they perceived as his tyrannical rule.

Second Triumvirate: The Second Triumvirate, comprising Octavian (later Augustus), Mark Antony, and Marcus Lepidus, was formed to avenge Caesar's assassination. Their actions led to the proscription of political enemies and the Battle of Philippi.

Battle of Actium: The Battle of Actium in 31 B.C. was a naval conflict between Octavian and Cleopatra on one side and Mark Antony on the other. Octavian's victory led to the end of the Ptolemaic Kingdom and the establishment of the Roman Empire.

Augustus (Octavian): Augustus, the first Roman Emperor, played a pivotal role in the transition from the Roman Republic to the Roman Empire. His reign, known as the Pax Romana, brought stability and prosperity to the empire.

Pax Romana: The Pax Romana, meaning "Roman Peace," refers to the long period of relative peace and stability that characterized the Roman Empire from 27 B.C. to 180 A.D.

Trajan: Trajan, one of the "Five Good Emperors," expanded the Roman Empire to its greatest territorial extent. His reign is often considered a high point in the history of the Roman Empire.

Marcus Aurelius: Marcus Aurelius, a philosopher-emperor, ruled during a challenging period marked by the Antonine Plague and military conflicts. His "Meditations" reflect his Stoic philosophy.

CHAPTER 9: BYZANTINE LEGACY

330 – 1453

Following the fall of the Western Roman Empire in the 5th century, the Roman Empire in the east, commonly known as the Byzantine Empire (referred to as the "Kingdom of the Romans" in its time), endured until 1453. Centred in Constantinople, its language and culture were Greek, and its predominant religion was Eastern Orthodox Christianity.

From the 4th century onwards, the Byzantine Empire's Balkan territories, including Greece, faced challenges from barbarian invasions. The Goths, Huns, and Slavic invasions in the 4th, 5th, and 7th centuries, respectively, led to a significant decline in imperial authority in the Greek peninsula. Following the Slavic invasion, the imperial government retained control primarily over islands and coastal areas, including key cities like Athens, Corinth, and Thessalonica, (Thessaloniki). Some mountainous regions maintained autonomy.

While there was limited Slavic settlement, the perception of a crisis of decline and depopulation in late antiquity is now considered outdated. Greek cities exhibited institutional continuity and prosperity between the 4th and 6th centuries A.D. In the early 6th century, Greece had around 80 cities, and the period from the 4th to the 7th century A.D. is regarded as one of high prosperity in Greece and the entire Eastern Mediterranean.

Until the 8th century, the Holy See of Rome governed almost all of modern Greece under the Pentarchy system. In the 8th century, Byzantine Emperor Leo III adjusted the jurisdiction of the Patriarchate of Constantinople.

The Byzantine recovery of lost provinces during the Arab–Byzantine wars began in the late 8th century, with most of the Greek peninsula returning to imperial control during the 9th century. This period saw a significant influx of Greeks from Sicily and Asia Minor, contributing to the region's stability and economic growth. The Greek Orthodox Church played a crucial role in disseminating Greek ideas to the wider Orthodox world during this time.

After the Fourth Crusade and the fall of Constantinople to the "Latins" in 1204, mainland Greece saw divisions between the Greek Despotate of Epirus and French rule (Frankokratia), with some islands under Venetian control. The re-establishment of the Byzantine imperial capital in Constantinople in 1261 resulted in the recovery of much of the Greek peninsula, although regional powers like the Frankish Principality of Achaea and the Greek Despotate of Epirus persisted into the 14th century. The islands remained under Genoese and Venetian influence.

During the Paleologi dynasty (1261–1453), a renewed sense of Greek patriotism emerged, accompanied by a reconnection with ancient Greek culture. Some proposed changing the imperial title to "Emperor of the Hellenes," and in the late 14th century, the emperor was often referred to as the "Emperor of the Hellenes" in international treaties.

The Conquest of Constantinople by The Crusaders

From 330 to 1453 A.D., Greece experienced a profound chapter in its history as it became an integral part of the Byzantine Empire, the Eastern Roman Empire that emerged from the division of the Roman Empire. The Byzantine Legacy left an enduring imprint on the cultural, religious, and political landscape of Greece, shaping its identity for centuries.

The establishment of Constantinople as the new capital of the Roman Empire by Emperor Constantine I in 330 A.D. marked a pivotal moment. The city, strategically located at the crossroads of Europe and Asia, became the heart of the

Byzantine Empire and a symbol of continuity with the Roman past. Byzantium, as it came to be known, served as a bastion of Roman governance and Hellenistic culture.

Under Byzantine rule, Greece became a vital province, known as the theme of Hellas. The administrative structure of the Byzantine Empire incorporated elements of Roman and Hellenistic governance, ensuring the continuity of local traditions while adapting to the needs of the imperial state.

The Byzantine Empire played a crucial role in preserving and transmitting classical Greek literature and philosophy. The works of ancient Greek scholars were diligently copied and preserved in Byzantine libraries, safeguarding the intellectual heritage of the Hellenistic world. Scholars like Michael Psellos and Anna Komnene continued the tradition of intellectual inquiry, contributing to philosophy, history, and rhetoric.

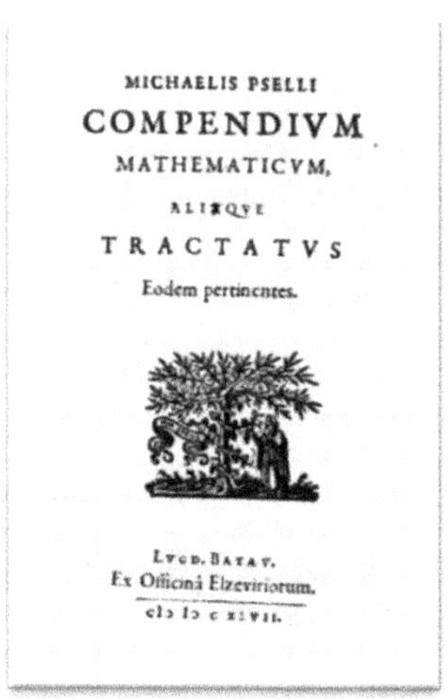

Michael Psellus's Compendium Mathematicum

Christianity played a central role in shaping the Byzantine identity. The conversion of Emperor Constantine to Christianity and the subsequent establishment of Christianity as the state religion transformed the religious landscape of the empire. The Ecumenical Councils, convened to address theological issues, left a lasting impact on Christian doctrine and influenced the development of Byzantine religious art and architecture.

Byzantine art and architecture, characterised by intricate mosaics, frescoes, and domed structures, reflected a fusion of Roman, Hellenistic, and Eastern influences. The Hagia Sophia, constructed under Emperor Justinian I in the 6th century, exemplified the grandeur of Byzantine architecture, becoming a masterpiece that symbolised the union of secular and religious power.

The Byzantine Empire faced external challenges, including invasions by various peoples such as Goths, Vandals, and Slavs. However, Byzantine military and diplomatic efforts, including the use of the thematic system, allowed the empire to endure and recover from setbacks.

The Byzantine legacy reached its height under the Macedonian Dynasty (867–1056 A.D.) and the Komnenian Dynasty (1081–1185 A.D.). During these periods, the empire experienced periods of cultural and economic prosperity, with Byzantine scholars contributing to the transmission of ancient knowledge to the West during the Renaissance.

The final chapter of the Byzantine Empire unfolded during the Palaiologan period, marked by external pressures from the Ottoman Turks. The fall of Constantinople in 1453, under the onslaught of Mehmed II, marked the end of the Byzantine Empire and the beginning of the Ottoman era.

The Byzantine Legacy profoundly influenced the course of Greek history. The Byzantine Empire transmitted the cultural and intellectual achievements of the Hellenistic world to subsequent generations. The Orthodox Christian faith, deeply rooted in Byzantine tradition, became a defining element of Greek identity. The legacy of Byzantine art, literature, and philosophy endured in the Greek consciousness, laying the groundwork for the cultural resilience that would shape Greece's future.

A SUMMARY OF KEY EVENTS, PEOPLE AND PLACES DURING THIS ERA

Constantine the Great: Constantine the Great, the first Christian Roman emperor, founded the city of Constantinople (modern-day Istanbul) in 330 A.D. This marked the beginning of the Byzantine Empire.

Justinian I: Justinian I, a Byzantine emperor, ruled from 527 to 565 A.D. and is renowned for his efforts to revive the Roman Empire. His codification of Roman laws, the construction of the Hagia Sophia, and military campaigns are notable aspects of his reign.

Theodora: Theodora, the wife of Justinian I, played a significant role in Byzantine politics. Her intelligence and influence were particularly evident during the Nika Riots, where she urged Justinian to remain steadfast.

Hagia Sophia: The Hagia Sophia, originally constructed by Constantine and later rebuilt by Justinian, stands as an architectural masterpiece. It served as a cathedral, mosque, and is now a museum.

Iconoclasm Controversy: The Iconoclasm Controversy, which spanned from the 8th to the 9th century, cantered on the veneration of religious icons. The debate over the use of religious images had significant religious and political implications.

Basil II: Basil II, also known as Basil the Bulgar Slayer, ruled from 976 to 1025 A.D. His reign saw the Byzantine Empire reach its territorial zenith, extending its influence in the Balkans and the Middle East.

Fourth Crusade: The Fourth Crusade, in 1204 A.D., resulted in the sacking of Constantinople by Crusader forces. This event had a profound impact on the Byzantine Empire, leading to the establishment of the Latin Empire.

Palaiologos Dynasty: The Palaiologos Dynasty, which ruled from 1259 to 1453 A.D., faced significant challenges, including invasions by the Ottoman Turks. The final emperor of the dynasty was Constantine XI.

Fall of Constantinople: In 1453, Constantinople fell to the Ottoman Turks, marking the end of the Byzantine Empire. The fall had far-reaching consequences for the history of the Mediterranean and the wider world.

Byzantine Art and Literature: Byzantine art and literature, characterised by intricate mosaics, illuminated manuscripts, and theological writings, played a crucial role in preserving and transmitting classical knowledge.

Byzantine Scholasticism: Byzantine scholars, such as Photios and Michael Psellos, contributed to Byzantine Scholasticism. They engaged in intellectual pursuits, including philosophy, theology, and classical studies.

Legacy of Orthodoxy: The Byzantine Empire played a crucial role in the development and preservation of Eastern Orthodox Christianity. The Byzantine legacy continues in the Eastern Orthodox Church, its traditions, and theological contributions.

Moving into the 14th century, significant portions of the Greek peninsula were lost by the Byzantine Empire to first the Serbs and then the Ottomans. By the early 15th century, the Ottoman advance left Byzantine territory in Greece mainly limited to Thessaloniki and the Peloponnese (Despotate of the Morea). After the fall of Constantinople in 1453, the Morea resisted Ottoman conquest until 1460, completing the Ottoman takeover of mainland Greece. Following the Turkish conquest, many Byzantine Greek scholars, responsible for preserving Classical Greek knowledge, fled to the West, contributing to the Renaissance.

The Byzantine castle of Angelokastro successfully repelled Ottoman sieges in Corfu in 1537, 1571, and 1716, forcing them to abandon plans to conquer the island. While most of mainland Greece and the Aegean islands came under Ottoman control by the late 15th century, Cyprus and Crete remained Venetian until 1571 and 1670, respectively. The Ionian Islands, the only part of the Greek-speaking world escaping long-term Ottoman rule, stayed Venetian until 1797, then passed to the United Kingdom in 1809 before unification with Greece in 1864.

The Ottoman conquest brought economic hardship to much of mainland Greece. Heavy taxes were imposed, and a policy of creating hereditary estates turned rural Greeks into serfs. The

Greek Orthodox Church and the Ecumenical Patriarchate of Constantinople were considered the ruling authorities of all Orthodox Christians in the Ottoman Empire, regardless of ethnicity. Discrimination against Christians and harsh treatment led to conversions to Islam, although some "crypto-Christians" returned to their old religious allegiance in the 19th century.

The Castle of Angelokastro

Ottoman administration of Greece varied, with arbitrary and often harsh measures. Some cities had governors appointed by the Sultan, while others were self-governed municipalities. Mountainous regions and many islands remained effectively autonomous.

Before the Greek Revolution of 1821, Greeks participated in various wars against the Ottomans, including the Battle of Lepanto in 1571, Epirus peasants' revolts of 1600–1601, the Morean War of 1684–1699, and the Orlov Revolt in 1770. These uprisings were suppressed with significant bloodshed. On the other side, many Greeks served in the Ottoman army, and the Ecumenical Patriarchate of Constantinople remained generally loyal to the empire.

The 16th and 17th centuries were considered a "dark age" in Greek history under Ottoman rule, with only the Ionian islands remaining free. Corfu resisted Ottoman sieges in 1537, 1571, and 1716. In the 18th century, a wealthy Greek merchant class emerged due to expertise in shipping and commerce. This diaspora, dominating trade within the Ottoman Empire, helped spread European intellectual movements, including ideas from the Reformation, Enlightenment, French Revolution, and romantic nationalism. In the late 18th century, Rigas Feraios, the first revolutionary envisioning an independent Greek state, published documents in Vienna related to Greek independence. However, he was murdered by Ottoman agents in 1798.

From 1453 to 1821, Greece endured a transformative period under Ottoman rule, witnessing centuries of Turkish dominance that reshaped its social, cultural, and political landscape. This era marked a complex interplay between the Ottoman Empire and the enduring Greek identity, as the Hellenic world navigated the challenges and adaptations brought about by this prolonged period of foreign rule.

Rigas Feraios

The Ottoman conquest of Constantinople in 1453 by Mehmed II marked a watershed moment, signifying the end of the Byzantine Empire and the beginning of Ottoman rule. Greece, with its rich cultural heritage and strategic significance, became an integral part of the Ottoman Empire.

Under Ottoman administration, Greece was organised into administrative units known as sanjaks, each governed by local officials appointed by the Ottoman central authority. The millet system allowed religious and ethnic communities, including the Orthodox Christian Greeks, to govern their own communal affairs. While this system provided a degree of autonomy, it also reinforced divisions between religious and ethnic groups.

The Greek Orthodox Church played a crucial role in preserving Greek language, culture, and identity during Ottoman rule. The clergy served as guardians of Greek traditions, maintaining schools and monastic institutions that became bastions of Hellenic culture. The survival of the Greek language and Orthodox Christian traditions became crucial components of Greek identity during this period.

Economic life under Ottoman rule underwent significant changes. The Greeks actively participated in trade, commerce, and artisanal activities within the Ottoman Empire and beyond. The diaspora of Greek merchants, known as the Phanariotes, became influential in the economic and political spheres, particularly in the Ottoman capital of Istanbul.

The Ottoman Empire, with its rich culture, also influenced Greek art, architecture, and cuisine. Architectural styles such as Ottoman classicism left their mark on urban planning and building design in Greek towns and cities. Culinary traditions, including dishes like baklava and moussaka, bear the imprint of Ottoman culinary influences.

The Greeks, however, were not passive subjects of Ottoman rule. Throughout the centuries, there were sporadic revolts and uprisings, expressing a yearning for autonomy and independence. The most notable of these was the Greek War of Independence, which began in 1821.

The cultural and intellectual life of the Greeks persisted during Ottoman rule, with scholars such as Adamantios Korais advocating for educational and linguistic reforms to revive classical Greek language and literature. The Enlightenment ideas of the 18th century, filtering into Greek intellectual circles, spurred a cultural revival known as the Greek Enlightenment.

The Statue of Adamantios Korais in Athens

Despite these cultural and economic achievements, the relationship between the Greek population and the Ottoman rulers was marked by periodic tensions and conflicts. The Janissaries, the Ottoman military elite, at times imposed heavy taxes and engaged in reprisals against the Greek population, leading to instances of social unrest.

The end of Ottoman rule in Greece was catalysed by the Greek War of Independence, which erupted in 1821. The struggle for independence, marked by notable events such as the Siege of Tripolitsa and the naval victories of the Greek fleet, ultimately led to the establishment of the modern Greek state in 1830.

The era of Ottoman rule left a complex legacy for Greece. While it posed challenges to Greek autonomy and cultural expression, it also became a crucible that forged aspects of the modern Greek identity. The Ottoman period laid the groundwork for the struggle for independence and the subsequent emergence of modern Greece as a sovereign nation-state.

A SUMMARY OF KEY EVENTS, PEOPLE AND PLACES DURING THIS ERA

Mehmed II (Mehmed the Conqueror): Mehmed II conquered Constantinople in 1453, marking the end of the Byzantine Empire. His reign saw the transformation of the city into the Ottoman capital, Istanbul.

Suleiman the Magnificent: Suleiman I, also known as Suleiman the Magnificent, ruled from 1520 to 1566. His reign was marked by military conquests, administrative reforms, and cultural flourishing. Suleiman is often considered one of the greatest Ottoman sultans.

Battle of Mohács: The Battle of Mohács in 1526 resulted in a decisive Ottoman victory over the Kingdom of Hungary. The battle had far-reaching consequences for the political landscape of Eastern Europe.

Selim II: Selim II, the son of Suleiman, ruled from 1566 to 1574. His reign faced challenges, including military defeats and economic issues, contributing to the gradual decline of Ottoman power.

The Siege of Vienna (1683): The Siege of Vienna in 1683 was a pivotal event in the Ottoman-Habsburg Wars. The Ottoman forces, led by Grand Vizier Kara Mustafa, were repelled by a coalition of European powers, marking the decline of Ottoman military dominance.

Treaty of Karlowitz: The Treaty of Karlowitz in 1699 marked the end of the Great Turkish War. It resulted in territorial losses for the Ottoman Empire in Eastern Europe, signalling the beginning of a period of decline.

Tanzimat Reforms: In the mid-19th century, the Tanzimat Reforms aimed at modernising the Ottoman Empire. These reforms addressed administrative, legal, and social structures in an attempt to strengthen the empire.

Mahmud II: Mahmud II, who ruled from 1808 to 1839, implemented key reforms during the Tanzimat period. His reign saw efforts to modernise the military, administrative apparatus, and legal system.

Greek War of Independence (1821–1829): The Greek War of Independence, starting in 1821, led to the establishment of the modern Greek state. The war marked the decline of Ottoman influence in the Balkans.

Janissaries Abolition: In 1826, Mahmud II initiated the abolition of the Janissaries, the elite Ottoman infantry. This move was part of broader efforts to modernise the Ottoman military.

Reforms of Abdulmejid I: Abdulmejid I, who ruled from 1839 to 1861, continued the Tanzimat reforms. His reign saw changes in education, administration, and the legal system.

Crimean War (1853–1856): The Crimean War, fought between the Ottoman Empire, Russia, and their respective allies, highlighted the Ottoman Empire's weakened state and contributed to further reform efforts.

CHAPTER 11: WAR OF INDEPENDENCE

1821 – 1830

The late eighteenth century had arrived and a surge in secular learning during the Modern Greek Enlightenment gave rise among Westernised Greek-speaking elites in the diaspora to the concept of a Greek nation with roots in ancient Greece. They perceived this nation as distinct from other Orthodox peoples and believed in its right to political autonomy. The Filiki Eteria, a secret organisation formed in Odessa in 1814 by merchants, was one such group. Claiming support from Tsarist Russia and drawing on the Orthodox messianic prophecy of resurrecting the eastern Roman Empire, the Filiki Eteria engaged traditional strata of the Greek Orthodox world in their liberal nationalist cause during an Ottoman trade crisis.

The Filiki Eteria Flag

The Filiki Eteria aimed to launch revolutions in the Peloponnese, the Danubian Principalities, and Constantinople. The first revolt, led by Alexandros Ypsilantis, started on 6 March 1821 in the Danubian Principalities but was quickly suppressed by the Ottomans. This event spurred the Greeks of the Peloponnese into action, and on 17 March 1821, the Maniots declared war on the Ottomans.

By the end of March, the Peloponnese was openly in revolt, and by October 1821, the Greeks, led by Theodoros Kolokotronis, had captured Tripolitsa. Revolts also occurred in Crete, Macedonia, and Central Greece, but they were soon quelled. The makeshift Greek navy achieved success against the Ottoman navy in the Aegean Sea, hindering Ottoman reinforcements by sea. In 1822 and 1824, the Turks and Egyptians ravaged the islands, committing massacres such as those on Chios and Psara. Approximately three-quarters of Chios' Greek population of 120,000 were killed, enslaved, or died of disease, galvanising public opinion in western Europe in favour of the Greek rebels.

Internal tensions led to two consecutive civil wars among different Greek factions. Meanwhile, Ottoman Sultan Mahmud II negotiated with Mehmet Ali of Egypt, who agreed to send his son Ibrahim Pasha to Greece to suppress the revolt in exchange for territorial gain. Ibrahim's success in the Peloponnese by the end of 1825, including the fall of Missolonghi in 1826, marked a turning point. Despite a defeat in Mani, Ibrahim had largely subdued the Peloponnesian revolt, and Athens had been retaken.

After years of negotiation, France, the Russian Empire, and the United Kingdom intervened in the conflict, sending naval forces to Greece. Learning of an imminent attack by the combined Ottoman-Egyptian fleets on the Greek island of Hydra, the allied fleet intercepted them at Navarino. The Battle of Navarino on 20 October 1827 resulted in the destruction of the Ottoman-Egyptian fleet. A French expeditionary force oversaw the evacuation of the Egyptian army from the Peloponnese, and the Greeks reclaimed the captured part of Central Greece by 1828.

From 1821 to 1830, Greece embarked on a courageous and arduous journey in the War of Independence, a historic struggle that ultimately led to the reclamation of its sovereignty and the establishment of the modern Greek state. This pivotal period marked the culmination of long-standing aspirations for freedom and autonomy, as the Greek people rose against Ottoman rule and sought to carve out a new chapter in their history.

The Greek War of Independence was ignited by a combination of factors, including the desire for national self-determination, the influence of Enlightenment ideals, and the enduring cultural and religious identity of the Greek Orthodox population. The revolution began in earnest on March 25, 1821, with the raising of the banner of independence in the Peloponnese.

The conflict unfolded in multiple theatres across Greece, with notable events such as the Massacre of Chios and the heroic stand at Missolonghi capturing the attention of the international community. The Greek revolutionaries, known as Filiki Eteria, displayed remarkable resilience and courage in the face of formidable Ottoman forces.

Key figures emerged as leaders in the struggle for Greek independence. Notable among them was Theodoros Kolokotronis, a military commander whose strategic brilliance played a crucial role in several victories, including the Battle of Dervenakia. Other leaders, such as Laskarina Bouboulina, Andreas Miaoulis, and Georgios Karaiskakis, contributed to both the military and political aspects of the revolution.

The Greek War of Independence gained international attention and garnered support from philhellenic movements in Europe. The London Protocol of 1827, signed by the Great Powers, recognised the need for Greek autonomy and called for an armistice. The naval Battle of Navarino in 1827, involving the fleets of Britain, France, and Russia, decisively weakened the Ottoman naval power, further tilting the balance in favour of the Greeks.

The culmination of these efforts came with the Treaty of Constantinople in 1830, which acknowledged the independence of Greece and outlined its borders. The establishment of the modern Greek state was formalised under the London Protocol of 1830, with Prince Otto of Bavaria chosen as the first King of Greece. The city of Nafplio was initially designated as the capital.

The Signing of the London Protocol in 1830

The Greek War of Independence left an indelible mark on the national psyche. The struggle for freedom and the sacrifices made by the Greek people became foundational elements of the emerging Greek identity. The narrative of the revolution and the heroic deeds of its leaders became integral components of Greek national consciousness.

The establishment of the modern Greek state, however, was not without challenges. Political and social complexities, including debates over the form of governance and territorial disputes, shaped the early years of the independent Greek state. Nevertheless, the War of Independence laid the groundwork for the development of a sovereign and self-governing Greece, marking the end of centuries of Ottoman rule and the beginning of a new era in Greek history.

Rigas Feraios: Rigas Feraios, a Greek writer and revolutionary, is considered a forerunner of the Greek War of Independence. His writings and efforts aimed at inspiring Greek independence.

Filiki Eteria: Filiki Eteria, or the Society of Friends, was a secret revolutionary organisation founded in 1814. It played a crucial role in coordinating the Greek War of Independence.

Alexander Ypsilantis: Alexander Ypsilantis, a leader of Filiki Eteria, initiated the Wallachian uprising in 1821. However, his campaign was met with limited success, and he eventually faced defeat.

The Massacres of Chios: The Massacres of Chios in 1822 involved brutal atrocities committed by Ottoman forces against the population of the island of Chios. The event drew international attention and support for the Greek cause.

Dimitrios Ypsilantis: Dimitrios Ypsilantis, brother of Alexander Ypsilantis, assumed leadership after his brother's defeat. He played a role in various battles during the early stages of the war.

Battle of Navarino (1827): The Battle of Navarino was a naval engagement between the Ottoman Empire and the allied forces of Britain, France, and Russia in 1827. It resulted in a decisive victory for the allies.

Lord Byron: Lord Byron, the British poet, volunteered and fought alongside the Greeks during the war. His financial and moral support contributed to the Greek cause, although he died in 1824.

Ioannis Kapodistrias: Ioannis Kapodistrias, a prominent Greek statesman, played a crucial role in securing diplomatic support for the Greek cause. He later became the first head of state of independent Greece.

Treaty of Adrianople (1829): The Treaty of Adrianople, signed in 1829, marked the end of the Greek War of Independence. It recognised the autonomy of Greece under Ottoman suzerainty.

First Hellenic Republic: Following the war, the First Hellenic Republic was established in 1828, with Ioannis Kapodistrias serving as its first president.

Battle of Petra (1829): The Battle of Petra in 1829 was a significant engagement during the final phase of the war, leading to the Ottoman recognition of Greek autonomy.

London Protocol (1830): The London Protocol of 1830 recognised Greece as an independent and sovereign state, effectively ending the formal hostilities of the Greek War of Independence.

In 1827, Ioannis Kapodistrias, hailing from Corfu, was selected by the Third National Assembly at Troezen as the inaugural governor of the First Hellenic Republic. Kapodistrias implemented a series of state, economic, and military institutions.

Ioannis Kapodistrias

However, tensions arose between him and local interests. Following his assassination in 1831 and the subsequent London conference a year later, the Great Powers—Britain, France, and Russia—installed Bavarian Prince Otto von Wittelsbach as monarch.

Bavarian Prince Otto von Wittelsbach Entering Athens

Otto's rule was autocratic, and during the first 11 years of Greece's independence, it was governed by a Bavarian oligarchy, initially led by Prime Minister Joseph Ludwig von Armansperg and later by Otto himself, who held the titles of both King and Premier. Greece remained under the influence of its protecting great powers—France, Russia, and the United Kingdom—alongside Bavaria. In 1843, an uprising compelled Otto to grant a constitution and a representative assembly.

Despite the absolutism of Otto's reign, the early years played a pivotal role in establishing institutions, building upon those initiated by Ioannis Kapodistrias, which continue to form the basis of Greek administration and education. Significant strides were made in areas such as the education system, maritime and postal communications, civil administration, and the legal code. This period saw historical revisionism focused on de-Byzantinification and de-Ottomanisation, emphasising the promotion of the country's Ancient Greek heritage. Reflecting this spirit, the national capital was relocated from Nafplio to Athens. Religious reform occurred, and the Church of Greece was established as the national church, even though Otto remained a Catholic. The day of Annunciation, 25 March, was chosen as the anniversary of the Greek War of Independence to reinforce the link between Greek identity and Orthodoxy.

Otto was deposed in the 23 October 1862 Revolution, driven by causes including the Bavarian-dominated government, heavy taxation, and a failed attempt to annex Crete from the Ottoman Empire. The catalyst for the revolt was Otto's dismissal of Konstantinos Kanaris from the Premiership. Prince Wilhelm (William) of Denmark replaced Otto in 1863, taking the name George I. A new Constitution in 1864 transformed Greece from a constitutional monarchy into a more democratic crowned republic.

In 1875, Charilaos Trikoupis introduced the concept of a parliamentary majority as a requirement for forming a government, limiting the monarchy's power to appoint minority governments of its preference. Corruption, coupled with Trikoupis' increased spending on infrastructure projects like the Corinth Canal, strained the weak Greek economy, leading to the declaration of public insolvency in 1893. Greece accepted the imposition of an International Financial Commission to enforce the repayment of the country's debtors.

Despite economic challenges, all Greeks were united in their determination to liberate Hellenic lands under Ottoman rule. The prolonged revolt in Crete from 1866 to 1869 heightened nationalist fervor. When war broke out between Russia and the Ottomans in 1877, Greek popular sentiment rallied to Russia's side, but Greece was too poor and concerned about British intervention to officially join the war. However, in 1881, Thessaly and small parts of Epirus were ceded to Greece as part of the Treaty of Berlin. Greeks in Crete continued to stage regular revolts, and in 1897, the Greek government, under Theodoros Deligiannis, declared war on the Ottomans.

The Greco-Turkish War of 1897 resulted in defeat for the poorly trained and equipped Greek army, but Greece lost only a small amount of territory to Turkey, while Crete became an autonomous state. With state coffers empty, fiscal policy came under International Financial Control. Concerned about the Ilinden uprising of the Internal Macedonian Revolutionary Organisation (IMRO) in 1903, the Greek government sponsored a guerrilla campaign in Ottoman-ruled Macedonia, known as the Macedonian Struggle, which ended with the Young Turk Revolution in 1908.

A Scene from The Greco-Turkish War of 1897

Amidst general dissatisfaction with the seeming inertia and unattainability of national aspirations under the premiership of the cautious reformist Theotokis, a group of military officers organised a coup in August 1909 and shortly thereafter called to Athens Cretan politician Eleftherios Venizelos, who conveyed a vision of national regeneration. After winning two elections and becoming Prime Minister in 1910, Venizelos initiated wide-ranging fiscal, social, and constitutional reforms, reorganised the military, made Greece a member of the Balkan League, and led the country through the Balkan Wars. By 1913, Greece's territory and population had almost doubled, annexing Crete, Epirus, and Macedonia.

Greece in the Balkan League

In the following years, the struggle between King Constantine I and charismatic Venizelos over the country's foreign policy on the eve of First World War dominated the country's political scene and divided the country into two opposing groups. During parts of WW1, Greece had two governments: A royalist pro-German one in Athens and a Venizelist pro-Entente one in Thessaloniki. The two governments were united in 1917, when Greece officially entered the war on the side of the Entente.

Amidst widespread dissatisfaction with the perceived inertia and unattainability of national aspirations under the premiership of the cautious reformist Theotokis, a group of military officers organised a coup in August 1909. Shortly thereafter, they summoned Cretan politician Eleftherios Venizelos to Athens, who conveyed a vision of national regeneration. After winning two elections and becoming Prime Minister in 1910, Venizelos initiated comprehensive fiscal, social, and constitutional reforms, reorganised the military, made Greece a member of the Balkan League, and led the country through the Balkan Wars. By 1913, Greece's territory and population had almost doubled, annexing Crete, Epirus, and Macedonia. In the subsequent years, the struggle between King Constantine I and charismatic Venizelos over the country's foreign policy on the eve of the First World War dominated the political scene, dividing the nation into two opposing groups. During parts of World War I, Greece had two governments: a royalist pro-German one in Athens and a Venizelist pro-Entente one in Thessaloniki. The two governments were united in 1917 when Greece officially entered the war on the side of the Entente.

World War I Poster in Greece

In the aftermath of World War I, Greece sought further expansion into Asia Minor, a region with a large native Greek population at the time. However, Greece was defeated in the Greco-Turkish War of 1919–1922, contributing to a massive flight of Asia Minor Greeks. These events coincided with the Greek genocide (1914–1922), during which, according to various sources, Ottoman and Turkish officials played a role in the death of several hundred thousand Asia Minor Greeks, along with similar numbers of Assyrians and a larger number of Armenians. The resulting Greek exodus from Asia Minor became permanent and expanded through an official population exchange between Greece and Turkey, part of the terms of the Treaty of Lausanne that concluded the war.

The subsequent era was marked by instability, as over 1.5 million propertyless Greek refugees from Turkey needed integration into Greek society. Cappadocian Greeks, Pontian Greeks, and non-Greek followers of Greek Orthodoxy were all subject to the exchange. Some refugees couldn't speak the language and were from unfamiliar environments, such as the Cappadocians and non-Greeks. The refugees also led to a significant post-war population increase, constituting more than a quarter of Greece's prior population.

From 1830 to 1922, Modern Greece underwent a transformative journey, transitioning from a newly established kingdom to the tumultuous period that culminated in the establishment of the Greek Republic. This era witnessed the consolidation of the Greek state, political developments, territorial expansions, and the challenges of nation-building, shaping the foundations of contemporary Greece.

The early years of the independent Greek state were marked by efforts to establish stable governance and define the parameters of the fledgling kingdom. Otto of Bavaria, the first king of Greece, faced challenges in navigating the complex socio-political landscape. His rule, marked by political tensions and conflicts with local factions, eventually led to his removal in 1862.

The period that followed, known as the Great Idea or Megali Idea, was characterised by aspirations to reunite territories with a Greek-speaking population under the banner of the Greek state. The incorporation of the Ionian Islands (1864) and Thessaly (1881) into the kingdom marked territorial expansions, bringing regions with Greek populations into the nation-state.

The late 19th century saw a series of political changes, including the establishment of a constitutional monarchy in 1864 and the adoption of a new constitution in 1864. The political landscape was marked by the emergence of political parties, such as the Liberal Party and the New Party, reflecting the evolving dynamics of Greek politics.

The Balkan Wars of 1912–1913 were pivotal moments in Greece's quest for territorial expansion. The successful military campaigns against the Ottoman Empire led to the acquisition of Epirus, Macedonia, Crete, and the Aegean Islands, realising aspects of the Megali Idea. The First World War further influenced Greece's position, with the country initially remaining neutral before entering the conflict on the side of the Allies.

The Treaty of Sèvres in 1920 held significant consequences for Greece. The envisioned expansion of Greek territories in Asia

Minor, however, faced challenges, leading to the Greco-Turkish War (1919–1922). The war culminated in the Asia Minor Disaster, with Greek forces retreating and a massive exchange of populations between Greece and Turkey under the Treaty of Lausanne in 1923.

King Constantine I

The Asia Minor Disaster had profound repercussions, including the influx of refugees into Greece and the destabilisation of the political and social fabric. King Constantine I abdicated in 1922, and Greece subsequently transitioned from a monarchy to a republic in 1924. The brief period of the Second Hellenic Republic faced internal strife and political instability, culminating in the establishment of a military dictatorship in 1936.

The Modern Greek era up to 1922 reflects the complexities of state-building, territorial aspirations, and the challenges of navigating international geopolitics. The quest for national unity, territorial integrity, and political stability remained ongoing themes that would continue to shape the trajectory of Greece in the years to come.

A SUMMARY OF KEY EVENTS, PEOPLE AND PLACES DURING THIS ERA

Ioannis Kapodistrias: Ioannis Kapodistrias, a prominent statesman and diplomat, served as the first head of state of independent Greece. His efforts included the establishment of a centralised government and diplomatic initiatives.

Otto of Greece: Otto, a Bavarian prince, became the first king of modern Greece in 1832. His reign saw challenges, including political turmoil and conflicts with the Greek people, leading to his eventual deposition in 1862.

Constitution of 1844: The Constitution of 1844 marked an important step in the development of constitutional government in Greece. It established a constitutional monarchy with a parliamentary system.

The Great Idea (Megali Idea): The Great Idea was a nationalist concept advocating the expansion of Greek territory to include areas with a significant Greek population. This idea influenced Greek foreign policy throughout the 19th and early 20th centuries.

Greek War of Independence (1866–1869): The Greek War of Independence against Ottoman rule in Crete and other regions took place between 1866 and 1869. It was part of the broader struggle for Greek irredentism.

Charilaos Trikoupis: Charilaos Trikoupis, a statesman and prime minister, played a crucial role in moderniseng Greece during the late 19th century. His tenure saw economic reforms, infrastructure development, and increased public education.

Balkan Wars (1912–1913): The Balkan Wars were a series of conflicts involving Greece, Serbia, Bulgaria, and Montenegro against the Ottoman Empire. The wars resulted in territorial gains for Greece, including parts of Macedonia.

Eleftherios Venizelos: Eleftherios Venizelos, a prominent politician and statesman, served multiple terms as Prime Minister. He played a key role in the Balkan Wars, negotiations at the Paris Peace Conference, and the modernisation of Greece.

World War I: Greece entered World War I on the side of the Allies in 1917. Political divisions and conflicts over Greece's involvement in the war contributed to instability.

National Schism: The National Schism was a period of political and social division in Greece during and after World War I. It involved conflicts between supporters of King Constantine I and supporters of Prime Minister Venizelos.

Treaty of Sèvres (1920): The Treaty of Sèvres, signed in 1920, outlined the post-World War I settlement in the Ottoman Empire and recognised significant territorial gains for Greece. However, the treaty was not fully implemented.

Asia Minor Campaign (1919–1922): The Asia Minor Campaign, also known as the Greco-Turkish War, was a conflict between Greece and the Turkish National Movement led by Mustafa Kemal Atatürk. The war ended in the Greek defeat and the exchange of populations between Greece and Turkey.

Treaty of Lausanne (1923): The Treaty of Lausanne, signed in 1923, officially ended the Greco-Turkish War. It established the modern borders between Greece and Turkey and marked the end of Greek irredentism.

CHAPTER 13: WORLD WARS AND BEYOND

1922 – 2000

The aftermath of the Asia Minor Disaster in 1922 left an enduring impact on Greek society. The influx of refugees, economic challenges, and political instability shaped the early years of the Second Hellenic Republic. In 1936, Greece faced another significant upheaval with the establishment of a military dictatorship led by Ioannis Metaxas. This regime, known as the 4th of August Regime, sought to impose order and enact nationalist policies.

Ioannis Metaxas

The onset of World War II brought further challenges for Greece. The Italian invasion in 1940 was met with Greek resistance, a pivotal moment that played a role in the broader context of the war. The subsequent German invasion in 1941 led to a brutal occupation, marked by resistance movements, guerrilla warfare, and the devastating impact of the Holocaust on Greek Jews. Greece's resistance against Axis forces and the struggle for liberation became emblematic of the country's resilience. The Battle of Crete in 1941 and the Greek Resistance movements, such as the National Liberation Front (EAM), played key roles in the broader struggle against Nazi occupation. The liberation of Greece in 1944 and the subsequent political developments laid the groundwork for the restoration of democratic governance.

The post-war period in Greece was characterised by political instability, marked by a series of changes in government and a polarised political climate. The Greek Civil War (1946–1949) between government forces and leftist guerrilla groups exacerbated divisions within Greek society. The conflict, fuelled by ideological and geopolitical factors, concluded with the defeat of the leftist forces and the establishment of political stability.

The latter half of the 20th century saw Greece undergoing significant economic and social transformations. King Constantine II's dismissal of George Papandreou's centrist government in July 1965 initiated a period of political turbulence, culminating in a coup d'état on 21 April 1967 by the Regime of the Colonels. Under the junta, civil rights were suspended, political repression intensified, and human rights abuses, including state-sanctioned torture, were rampant. Economic growth remained rapid until plateauing in 1972. The brutal suppression of the Athens Polytechnic uprising on 17 November 1973 set in motion events that led to the fall of the Papadopoulos regime, resulting in a counter-coup overthrowing Georgios Papadopoulos and establishing Brigadier Dimitrios Ioannidis as the new junta strongman. On 20 July 1974, Turkey invaded Cyprus in response to a Greek-backed Cypriot coup, triggering a political crisis in Greece that led to the regime's collapse and the restoration of democracy through Metapolitefsi.

The former Prime Minister Konstantinos Karamanlis returned from self-exile in Paris in 1974, marking the beginning of the Metapolitefsi era. The first multiparty elections since 1964 were held on the first anniversary of the Polytechnic uprising. A democratic and republican constitution was promulgated on 11 June 1975 following a referendum that chose not to restore the monarchy. Meanwhile, Andreas Papandreou, the son of George Papandreou, founded the Panhellenic Socialist Movement (PASOK) in response to Karamanlis's conservative New Democracy party, with the two political formations dominating government over the next four decades. Greece rejoined NATO in 1980.

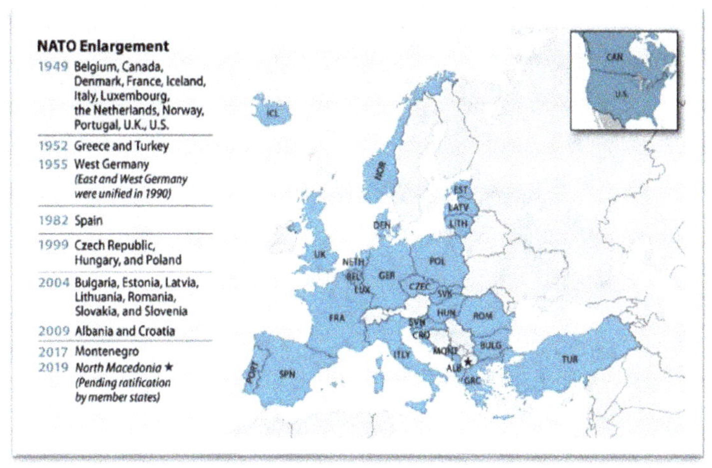

The History of NATO Membership

Greece became the tenth member of the European Communities (subsequently subsumed by the European Union) on 1 January 1981, ushering in a period of sustained growth. Widespread investments in industrial enterprises and heavy infrastructure, along with funds from the European Union and growing revenues from tourism, shipping, and a fast-growing service sector, raised the country's standard of living to unprecedented levels.

In 1981, the election of Andreas Papandreou resulted in significant reforms throughout the 1980s. Among other changes, he recognised the national resistance during World War Two, civil marriage was introduced, the dowry was abolished, and the education system and foreign policy doctrines changed. However, Papandreou's tenure was also associated with corruption, double-digit inflation, stagnation, and budget deficits that caused problems in the Greek economy later on.

Greece in the European Union

From 1922 to 2000, Greece navigated a tumultuous journey through the events of the 20th century, marked by geopolitical shifts, conflicts, political transitions, and moments of societal upheaval. This era witnessed Greece's involvement in both World Wars, periods of political turbulence, and its eventual integration into the European Union, reflecting the complexities of the modern Greek experience. The 20th century witnessed Greece grappling with the complexities of war, occupation, political transitions, and economic transformations. The resilience of the Greek people and the nation's ability to adapt to changing circumstances reflect the multifaceted nature of Greece's modern historical narrative. The country's journey from the aftermath of World War I to its role in the European Union encapsulates the dynamic interplay of internal and external forces that have shaped Greece into the 21st century.

Greek Republic (1924–1935): After the Asia Minor Campaign and the defeat in 1922, Greece transitioned to a republic in 1924. This period saw political instability, economic difficulties, and the eventual restoration of the monarchy in 1935.

Metaxas Regime: Ioannis Metaxas, a military officer, established an authoritarian regime in Greece in 1936. The Metaxas regime ruled until the Italian invasion in 1940.

Greco-Italian War (1940–1941): The Greco-Italian War began in 1940 when Italy, led by Benito Mussolini, invaded Greece. The Greek forces successfully resisted the invasion, marking a rare victory against Axis aggression during the early stages of World War II.

German Occupation (1941–1944): During World War II, Greece fell under Axis occupation, primarily by German forces. The occupation brought significant hardships, including famine and resistance activities.

Greek Resistance: The Greek Resistance, composed of various groups, played a key role in opposing Axis occupation. The resistance contributed to the liberation of Greece and the downfall of the Axis powers.

Civil War (1946–1949): The Greek Civil War erupted in 1946 between the government forces (supported by the West) and communist insurgents. The conflict concluded with the defeat of the communists in 1949.

Marshal Plan and Economic Recovery: Greece benefited from the Marshall Plan, a U.S. initiative for post-war reconstruction. The economic aid contributed to Greece's recovery and development in the post-war period.

Constantine Karamanlis: Constantine Karamanlis, a statesman, played a crucial role in Greek politics. He served as Prime Minister and later as President, overseeing key reforms and the country's entry into the European Economic Community (EEC).

Military Junta (1967–1974): A military junta, led by Colonel Georgios Papadopoulos, seized power in a coup in 1967. The junta ruled until its downfall in 1974, following the Cyprus crisis.

Cyprus Crisis (1974): The Cyprus Crisis in 1974, triggered by a coup and the Turkish invasion of Cyprus, had significant implications for Greek-Turkish relations. It resulted in the division of Cyprus.

Return to Democracy (1974): Following the fall of the military junta, Greece transitioned back to democracy in 1974. This period saw the restoration of the monarchy and its subsequent abolition, establishing Greece as a republic.

Papandreou Family Influence: The Papandreou family, including Andreas Papandreou and his son George Papandreou, played prominent roles in Greek politics. Both served as Prime Ministers and contributed to political and economic developments.

Entry into the European Union (1981): Greece joined the European Economic Community (EEC), the predecessor to the European Union, in 1981. EU membership brought economic benefits and further integration into European institutions.

1990s Economic Challenges: The 1990s were marked by economic challenges, including high inflation and public debt. Greece implemented economic reforms to address these issues.

2000 – PRESENT

In the 1990s and 2000s, Greek influence in the Balkan countries reached its peak. The country adopted the euro in 2001 and successfully hosted the 2004 Summer Olympic Games in Athens.

Beginning in 2010, Greece suffered substantially from the Great Recession and the related European sovereign debt crisis. Due to the adoption of the euro, Greece, when experiencing a financial crisis, could no longer devalue its currency to regain competitiveness. Youth unemployment was especially high during this period. In the two elections of May and June 2012, there was a major change in the political landscape of Greece, with new parties emerging from the collapse of the popularity of the two main parties of the past, PASOK and New Democracy. In January 2015, Alexis Tsipras was elected as prime minister, becoming the first prime minister of Greece outside the two main political parties. This Greek government-debt crisis and subsequent austerity policies resulted in protests and social strife. The crisis is generally considered to have ended around 2018, with the conclusion of the bailout mechanisms and the return of economic growth.

Simultaneously, in June 2018, the leaders of Greece, Alexis Tsipras, and North Macedonia, Zoran Zaev, signed the Prespa

Agreement, resolving the naming dispute that strained relations between the two countries and easing the latter's path to becoming a member of the EU and NATO.

In July 2019, Kyriakos Mitsotakis became Greece's new prime minister after his centre-right New Democracy party won the election over the ruling leftist Syriza. In March 2020, Greece's parliament elected a non-partisan candidate, Katerina Sakellaropoulou, as the first female President of Greece. During the 2020s, the Greek economy continues to rebound, as a result of post-COVID economic recovery, robust investments, and an increase in tourist revenues and consumer spending.

From the start of the 21st century to the present, Greece has faced a myriad of challenges and triumphs, navigating a complex landscape shaped by economic crises, political transformations, and ongoing efforts to address social and environmental concerns. This contemporary era reflects Greece's resilience, adaptability, and ongoing quest for stability and progress.

The early years of the 21st century were marked by economic challenges, culminating in the global financial crisis of 2008. Greece, already grappling with fiscal issues, faced a severe economic downturn that led to a sovereign debt crisis. The subsequent austerity measures imposed by international creditors and the European Union sparked widespread protests and social unrest, creating a profound impact on the Greek economy and society.

The economic crisis prompted political changes in Greece. The rise of new political movements, including Syriza, reflected a shift in public sentiment and a desire for alternative approaches to economic governance. The election of Alexis Tsipras as Prime Minister in 2015 marked a significant moment in Greek politics, with efforts to renegotiate Greece's relationship with its creditors and address the impacts of austerity.

Alexis Tsipras as Prime Minister in 2015

Greece's journey through the economic crisis has been intertwined with its role in the European Union. Negotiations over bailout packages, structural reforms, and the terms of Greece's membership in the Eurozone underscored the complexities of balancing national sovereignty with European integration. The subsequent stabilising of the Greek economy and the gradual emergence from the financial crisis represented a testament to the resilience of the Greek people. The ongoing refugee and migration crisis has also played a prominent role in shaping Greece's contemporary narrative. The influx of refugees, particularly from conflict zones in the Middle East, posed humanitarian challenges and prompted debates about Greece's role in managing the crisis within the broader European context.

Environmental concerns have gained prominence in contemporary Greece. The country has grappled with issues such as deforestation, wildfires, and the impact of climate change. Efforts to address environmental sustainability and conservation have become integral components of national policies and international collaborations.

Greece's geopolitical role has been significant, particularly in the Eastern Mediterranean. Energy exploration, territorial disputes, and diplomatic relations with neighboring countries have been focal points of Greece's foreign policy considerations.

The COVID-19 pandemic, starting in 2019, has posed unprecedented challenges globally, and Greece has not been exempt. The country has navigated the complex landscape of public health responses, economic implications, and societal adjustments in the face of the pandemic.

Despite the challenges, Greece has witnessed moments of triumph. The successful hosting of the Athens 2004 Summer

Olympics showcased the country's ability to organise and execute a major international event. Cultural achievements, archaeological discoveries, and tourism initiatives have also contributed to Greece's positive global image.

The Olympics in Greece 2004

Contemporary Greece stands at the intersection of tradition and modernity, navigating the complexities of a rapidly changing world. The resilience and adaptability of the Greek people, coupled with ongoing efforts to address economic, social, and environmental challenges, highlight Greece's determination to shape its future while remaining deeply rooted in its rich historical and cultural heritage.

Entry into the Eurozone (2001): In 2001, Greece officially adopted the euro as its currency, signalling further integration into the European Union and the Eurozone.

2004 Athens Olympics: Greece hosted the Summer Olympics in Athens in 2004. The event showcased the country's cultural heritage and modern capabilities, but it also brought attention to economic concerns.

Financial Crisis (2008–2009): Greece faced a severe financial crisis in 2008–2009, leading to economic recession and significant social repercussions. The country received bailout packages from international creditors, triggering austerity measures.

Bailouts and Austerity: Greece received financial assistance from the International Monetary Fund (IMF), European Central Bank (ECB), and the European Commission (EC) in a series of bailout programs. Austerity measures were implemented to address economic challenges.

Debt Crisis and Protests: The austerity measures led to widespread protests and social unrest in Greece. Demonstrations, strikes, and public dissatisfaction became prominent features of the country's response to the economic crisis.

Syriza Government (2015–2019): The left-wing Syriza party, led by Alexis Tsipras, came to power in 2015. The government faced challenges in negotiating with international creditors and implementing reforms while addressing public concerns.

Prespa Agreement (2018): The Prespa Agreement, signed in 2018, resolved the longstanding naming dispute between

Greece and North Macedonia. The agreement facilitated improved diplomatic relations between the two countries.

Exit from Bailout Programs (2018): Greece officially exited its third international bailout program in 2018, marking the end of the formal financial assistance programs. However, economic challenges and reforms continued.

Response to COVID-19 Pandemic: Greece, like the rest of the world, faced challenges posed by the COVID-19 pandemic. The government implemented measures to control the spread of the virus and mitigate its impact on public health and the economy.

New Democracy Government (2019–present): The New Democracy party, led by Kyriakos Mitsotakis, came to power in 2019. The government has focused on economic reforms, attracting foreign investment, and addressing issues such as migration.

East Mediterranean Tensions: Tensions in the East Mediterranean have arisen due to disputes over maritime boundaries and energy resources. Greece has been involved in discussions with neighbouring countries and international actors to address these issues.

Migration Challenges: Greece has faced challenges related to migration, particularly with an influx of refugees and asylum seekers. The situation has prompted discussions on EU migration policies and humanitarian concerns.

ANCIENT GREECE:

Solon (c. 640–c. 560 B.C.):

- Known for legal and political reforms in Athens.

Cleisthenes (c. 570–c. 508 B.C.):

- Considered the father of Athenian democracy.

Pericles (c. 495–429 B.C.):

- Prominent Athenian statesman during the Golden Age.

CLASSICAL AND HELLENISTIC PERIOD:

Alexander the Great (356–323 B.C.):

- Conqueror of a vast empire, including Greece.

ROMAN AND BYZANTINE PERIOD:

Constantine the Great (c. 272–337):

- Founder of Constantinople and the Byzantine Empire.

Justinian I (482–565):

- Notable for codifying Roman law in the Byzantine Empire.

OTTOMAN RULE:

Mehmed II (Mehmed the Conqueror) (1444–1446, 1451–1481):

- Conquered Constantinople in 1453, ending Byzantine Rule.

Suleiman I (Suleiman the Magnificent) (1520–1566):

-An influential Ottoman Sultan; expanded Ottoman territories.

Kara Mustafa Pasha (1676–1683):

- Led the unsuccessful Siege of Vienna in 1683.

Ali Pasha of Ioannina (Late 18th to early 19th century):

- Influential Ottoman ruler in western Greece.

Mahmud Dramali Pasha (1822–1823):

- Involved in the Ottoman response to the Greek War of Independence.

MODERN GREECE (POST-INDEPENDENCE):

Ioannis Kapodistrias (1776–1831):

- First head of state after the War of Independence.

Otto of Greece (1815–1867):

- First modern King of Greece, reigned from 1832 to 1862.

George I (1845–1913):

- Reigned as King of Greece from 1863 to 1913.

20th CENTURY:

Eleftherios Venizelos (1864–1936):

- Dominant political figure in early 20th-century Greece.

George II (1890–1947):

- King of Greece during parts of the 20th century.

POST-WORLD WAR II:

Konstantinos Tsaldaris (1884–1970):

- Prime Minister in the post-war period.

Andreas Papandreou (1919–1996):

- Founding leader of the PASOK party and Prime Minister.

Konstantinos Karamanlis (1907–1998):

- Prime Minister and later President; played a key role in shaping modern Greece.

Kostas Karamanlis (b. 1956):

- Prime Minister in the early 21st century.

Alexis Tsipras (b. 1974):

- Leader of SYRIZA; served as Prime Minister from 2015 to 2019.

Kyriakos Mitsotakis (b. 1968):

- Current Prime Minister; assumed office in July 2019.

This list covers a range of leaders from different historical periods in Greece. Keep in mind that political structures and titles may vary across time, and the dates provided are approximate.

TOP 25 FIGURES IN GREECE'S HISTORY

1. **Homer (c. 8th century B.C.):**

  - Author of the "Iliad" and the "Odyssey," foundational works of Greek literature.

2. **Heraclitus (c. 535–475 B.C.):**

  - Pre-Socratic philosopher known for his doctrine of change.

3. **Leonidas I (c. 540–480 B.C.):**

  - King of Sparta, led Spartans at the Battle of Thermopylae.

4. **Miltiades (c. 550–489 B.C.):**

  - Athenian general, commanded at the Battle of Marathon.

5. **Sophocles (c. 496–406 B.C.):**

  - Playwright, one of the three great tragedians of ancient Greece.

6. **Pericles (c. 495–429 B.C.):**

  - Prominent Athenian statesman during the Golden Age.

7. **Socrates (469–399 B.C.):**

  - Philosopher, key figure in the development of Western philosophy.

8. **Demosthenes (384–322 B.C.):**

  - Athenian statesman and orator.

9. **Aristotle (384–322 B.C.):**

  - Philosopher, student of Plato.

10. **Alexander the Great (356–323 B.C.):**

  - King of Macedonia, conqueror of a vast empire.

11. **Archimedes (c. 287–212 B.C.):**

  - Mathematician, physicist, and engineer.

12. **Cleopatra VII (69–30 B.C.):**

  - Last Pharaoh of Egypt.

13. **Saint Paul (c. 5–67 A.D.):**

- Early Christian missionary.

14. **Constantine the Great (c. 272–337)**:

   - Roman Emperor, founder of Constantinople.

15. **Byzantine Emperor Justinian I (482–565)**:

   - Justinian I, codifier of Roman law.

16: **Byzantine Emperor Theodora (c. 500–548)**:

   - Theodora, influential figure.

17. **Ioannis Kapodistrias (1776–1831)**:

   - First head of state after the Greek War of Independence.

18. **Lord Byron (1788–1824)**:

   - Philhellene poet, supporter of the Greek War of Independence.

19. **Odysseas Elytis (1911–1996)**:

   - Nobel Prize-winning poet.

20. **Melina Mercouri (1920–1994)**:

   - Acclaimed actress and politician.

21. **Ioannis Metaxas (1871–1941)**:

   - Prime Minister of Greece.

22. **Eleftherios Venizelos (1864–1936)**:

   - Prominent statesman in modern Greece.

23. **Aeschylus (c. 525–456 B.C.)**:

   - Early playwright, "Father of Tragedy."

24. **Hippocrates (c. 460–370 B.C.)**:

   - "Father of Medicine," influential physician.

25. **Alexis Tsipras (b. 1974)**:

   - Modern political figure, leader of SYRIZA.

This list gives an overview of the top 25 significant figures in Greek history covering philosophy, literature, art and politics.

IMAGE CREDITS

The Franchthi Cave	Efitsif via Wikimedia Commons
King Agamemnon	Public domain, via Wikimedia Commons
Archaeological excavations at Knossos	Zde, via Wikimedia Commons
The God Zeus Battling Typhon	William Blake, CC0, via Wikimedia Commons
The Bust of Homer	British Museum, Public domain, via Wikimedia Commons
Bronze Statue of the Warrier Sparta	Mary Harrsch, via Wikimedia Commons
Scene at the Battle of Marathon	John Steeple Davis, Public domain, via Wiki Commons
The Visionary Statesman Pericles	Vatican Museums, Public domain, via Wiki Commons
The Parthenon	Frederic Edwin Church, via Wikimedia Commons
King of Sparta at the Court of Archidamas by Thucydides	Hans Leonhard Schäufelein, via Wikimedia Commons
Alexander the Great	British Museum, Public domain, via Wikimedia Commons
Battle of Gaugamela	Charles Le Brun, via Wikimedia Commons
Ptolemy II	Naples National Archaeological Museum, via Wikimedia Commons
Roman Emperor Augustus	Szilas, Public domain, via Wikimedia Commons
Roman Emperor Constantine I	Internet Archive Book Images, No restrictions, via Wikimedia Commons
The Conquest of Constantinople by The Crusaders	David Aubert, Public domain, via Wikimedia Commons
Michael Psellus's Compendium Mathematicum	Biblioteca Europea di Informazione e Cultura, Public domain, via Wikimedia Commons
The Castle of Angelokastro	Dr.K. via Wikimedia Commons
Rigas Feraios	Andreas Kriezis, Public domain, via Wikimedia Commons
The Statue of Adamantios Korais in Athens	Georgios Vroutos, via Wikimedia Commons
The Filiki Eteria Flag	Philly boy92, Public domain, via Wikimedia Commons
The Signing of the London Protocol in 1830	Ludwig Michael von Schwanthaler, Public domain, via Wikimedia Commons
Ioannis Kapodistrias	National historical Museum, Athens, Public domain, via Wikimedia Commons
Bavarian Prince Otto von Wittelsbach Entering Athens	Public Domain in Wikipedia
A Scene from The Greco-Turkish War of 1897	P. Romagnoli and S. Zaniboni, Public domain, via Wikimedia Commons
Greece in the Balkan League	www.historycrunch.com
World War I Poster in Greece	Petros Roumbos, Public domain, via Wikimedia Commons
King Constantine I	Philip de László, Public domain, via Wikimedia Commons
Ioannis Metaxas	The Archaeological Society at Athens Public domain, via Wikimedia Commons
The History of NATO Membership	Paul Belkin, Public domain, via Wikimedia Commons
Greece in the European Union	Public Domain via Wikipedia Commons
Alexis Tsipras as Prime Minister in 2015	Arne Müseler, via Wikimedia Commons
The Olympics in Greece 2004	IOC, Public domain, via Wikimedia Commons

ABOUT THE AUTHOR

Martin Miller-Yianni, a London native born in 1958, emerged from a humble working-class background. Despite starting his career as a primary school teacher, an unexpected turn of events led him to venture into Southeastern Europe in 2005. Since then, Martin has fully embraced the unique way of life and culture of the region, igniting a passion for writing within him. Having served as a journalist and researcher for a leading information website about this area, he has developed a profound knowledge, understanding, and first-hand experience of this part of the world. Martin's intimate connection with Southeastern Europe, rooted in both personal and professional experiences, continues to inspire and influence his literary pursuits. His latest literary work on Greece is a testament to his deep appreciation and admiration for the region's rich and captivating heritage.

365 Bulgarian Adventures
(2006)
Publication Pending

26 Tales of Humanities Trials
(2023)
ISBN
978-619-92494-8-2

Simple Treasures in Bulgaria
(2008)
ISBN
978-0-9559-8490-7

I'm Bad at Poems
(2022)
ISBN
978-619-92494-2-0

Bulgaria Through the Ages
(2023)
ISBN
978-1-4476-2777-7

Redemption of Love
(2023)
ISBN
978-619-92494-0-6

100 Essential Recipes from Bulgaria
(2011)
ISBN
978-1-4477-0260-3

Romania Through the Ages
(2023)
ISBN
978-619-7742-19-0

North Macedonia Through the Ages
(2023)
ISBN
978-619-7742-25-1

Cyprus Through the Ages
(2023)
ISBN
978-619-7742-22-0